Collaborative Governance in Extractive Industries in Africa

The United Nations University Institute for Natural Resources in Africa (UNU-INRA), the only Institute of the United Nations University system based in Africa, was established in 1986. The Institute's mission is to empower African universities and other research institutions through capacity strengthening. UNU-INRA operates mainly from its headquarters in Accra, and Operating Units (OUs) - currently based at universities in Cameroon, Cote d'Ivoire, Namibia, Senegal and Zambia.

Institute for Natural Resources in Africa (UNU-INRA)
Second floor, International House, Annie Jiagge Road,
University of Ghana, Legon Campus
Accra, Ghana

Private Mail Bag, Kotoka International Airport,
Accra, Ghana

Email: *inra@unu.edu or unuinra@gmail.com*
www.inra.unu.edu

UNITED NATIONS
UNIVERSITY
UNU-INRA
Institute for Natural
Resources in Africa

Collaborative Governance in Extractive Industries in Africa

Edited by: Timothy Afful-Koomson

Kwabena Owusu Asubonteng

Collaborative Governance in Extractive Industries in Africa

Edited by: Timothy Afful-Koomson and Kwabena Owusu Asubonteng

© United Nations University Institute for Natural Resources in Africa (UNU-INRA), 2013

ISBN 978 – 9988 – 633 – 13 – 4

Cover design and layout: Kwabena O. Asubonteng

Cover photo credits: Yasuko Kusakari, David Mwinfang, Tullow Oil and UNU-INRA

Printed by Pixedit Limited, Ghana - 0203339269 | 0206893271

Disclaimer:

Table of Contents

List of Figures

List of Tables

Foreword

Large deposits of some of the major extractive resources such as gold, diamond, bauxite, uranium, copper and crude oil are found in Africa. With the discovery and development of new reserves, the continent has the potential of increasing its share of global commodity exports. The potential increase in market share coupled with the strong price performance of major commodities that is expected to continue over the next decade should present great opportunities for African countries to make significant progress towards inclusive growth.

It has been demonstrated by most countries that have been successful in using revenues from extractive industries to transform their economies and to lift greater percentage of their population from poverty that improved transparency and efficient management of the revenue is critical. Improved transparency and efficient management of revenues from extractive industries will not be achieved without a governance system that is itself transparent, legitimate, inclusive, (of key stakeholders) and accountable.

With increasing globalisation and emergence of development paradigms such as the green economy, African countries endowed with extractive resources cannot afford to allow protracted conflicts to undermine the transformative impacts of their extractive industries. Some emerging countries are also becoming active players in the African extractive industries and in the international commodity markets. African countries cannot afford to continue signing extractive resource contracts with these emerging countries without strengthening their governance systems. They cannot afford to allow fragile governance systems to encourage rent-seeking behaviours such as corruption and mismanagement of revenues from extractive industries. This cannot continue while a greater percentage of the population live in poverty and natural resources are depleted, polluted and rendered worthless for future generation.

I am happy that the United Nations University (UNU) through its Institute for Natural Resources in Africa (UNU-INRA) has recognised the value of good governance of extractive industries and is committed to contributing to the knowledge necessary to make this happen in Africa. The initiative to improve governance and management of extractive industries encompass the key issues under UNU's thematic area of Development Governance. This book which is part of that initiative is also consistent with UNU-INRA's mission to facilitate the generation of evidence-based knowledge to inform and empower leaders and relevant stakeholders for policy and decisions that will add value to Africa's natural resources and improve the livelihoods of its population.

It is worthwhile to reiterate what Kofi Annan - former Secretary-General of the United Nations said in the African Progress Report 2013. "African governments must rise to the challenges posed by fiscal policy, tax reform and the development of industrial policies. They must manage their countries' oil, gas and mining resources efficiently and share revenues fairly. For too long, African governments have been responding to externally driven transparency agendas. They have been following, not leading. And it is time to change this pattern".

This book will be of great benefit to African governments who want to lead by formulating strategic governance frameworks to improve resolution of conflicts between key stakeholders of extractive resources. It will provide useful information about the critical elements that those countries should consider in their efforts to improve governance and consequently enhance the transparency of extractive resource contracts between governments and corporations. Improved governance regime will also help revenue administration agencies to be more accountable and efficient in the collection, distribution and management of fees, taxes and royalties from extractive industries. This book will also be of value to development practitioners, the private sector, bilateral and multilateral donors with key interest in improving governance of extractive industries in Africa and in other developing countries.

I am confident that collaborative governance of extractive industries in Africa will contribute to the efforts to use revenues from extractive resources for inclusive growth. As indicated in this book, only countries, which can strategically implement applicable elements of collaborative governance that will realise some of the values discussed in the book. UNU-INRA is committed to working with governments in Africa to formulate and implement some of the recommendations that will be applicable to their particular situation.

David M. MALONE

Rector,

United Nations University

Acknowledgements

This book is a knowledge product from the International Conference on Sustainable Development of Natural Resources in Africa, 2011 which marked the 25th anniversary of the United Nations University Institute for Natural Resources in Africa (UNU-INRA). The book has become a reality due to the joint efforts of several groups. The conference was conceptualised and organised by the staff (academic and administrative) of UNU-INRA under the able leadership of Dr. Elias T. Ayuk, Director of UNU-INRA. To Prof. Konrad Osterwalder, former Rector of United Nations University, a big thank you for the continued intellectual and moral support to the Institute during the pre-conference and conference periods.

We are grateful to Dr. Kwadwo Tutu, Dr. Frank K. Nyame, Dr. Paulette Bynoe, Dr. Inge Amundsen, Dr. Joe Asamoah, Dr. Abdulai Darimani and Ms Madonna Afiba Dolphyne for their academic papers and poster contributions to theme two of the conference *"enhancing collaborative governance and management of the extractive industries for equitable wealth distribution and environmental management in Africa"*, which is the focus of this book. It has been a wonderful experience working with you. These papers, after a rigorous review, are a major part of this book. We also wish to extend our sincere gratitude to the chair persons, Dr. Joyce Aryee and Dr. Stephen Duah Yentumi and their respective rapporteurs, Prof. Stephen Simukanga, and Dr. Binate Fofana for steering the discussion under this theme. Also to the panellists of the discussion - Dr. Obijiofor Aginam, Dr. Sebastian Dessus, Paul Sowley, Dr. Anthony Aubyn and Nana Oye Mansa Yeboaa I, we appreciate your contributions to the fruitful dialogue during the plenary session.

Finally, we are grateful to all the participants who converged at the conference to share their knowledge and experiences for the advancement of sustainable resource management in Africa, and to all who have contributed in diverse ways in making the publication of this book possible.

List of Abbreviations

AIMES	African Initiative on Mining, Environment and Society
API	American Petroleum Institute
APRM	African Peer Review Mechanism
ASM	Artisanal Small-scale Mining
CASM	Communities and Artisanal and Small-Scale Mining
CBO	Community-Based Organisation
CDF	Community Development Funds
COMESA	Common Market for Eastern and Southern Africa
CPI	Corruption Perception Index (of Transparency International)
CSO	Civil Society Organisation
CSR	Corporate Social Responsibility
DRC	Democratic Republic of Congo
ECA	United Nations Economic Commission for Africa
ECCAS	Economic Community of Central African States
ECLAC	United Nations Economic Commission for Latin America and the Caribbean
ECOWAS	Economic Community of West African States
EIA	Environmental Impact Assessment
EIR	Extractive Industries Review
EI	Extractive Industries
EITI	Extractive Industries Transparency Initiative
EMP	Environmental Management Plan

EMS	Environmental Management System
EPA	Environmental Protection Agency
ESIA	Environmental and Social Impact Assessment
FDI	Foreign Direct Investment
GDP	Gross Domestic Product
GGMC	Guyana Geology and Mines Commission
GNPC	Ghana National Petroleum Corporation
GPI	Global Reporting Initiative
ha	Hectare
HDPE	High Density Polythene
HIPC	Highly Indebted Poor Country
IBA	Impact and Benefit Agreement
ICMM	International Council on Mining and Metals
ICSDNRA	International Conference on Sustainable Development of Natural resources in Africa
IIED	International Institute for Environment and Development
IMF	International Monetary Fund
IUCN	International Union for Conservation of Nature
KPCS	Kimberley Process Certification Scheme
km	kilometre
LSM	Large-Scale Mining
MMSD	Mining, Minerals and Sustainable Development Project
NCOM	National Coalition of Mining (Ghana)
NEAP	National Environmental Action Plan (Guyana)
NEPAD	New Partnership for Africa's Development
NGO	Non-Governmental Organisation

NNPC	Nigerian National Petroleum Corporation
NPM	New Public Management
OBI	Open Budget Institute
OECD	Organisation for Economic Co-operation and Development
PPP	Public-Private Partnership
PSA	Production Sharing Agreement
PSC	Production Sharing Contract
PRSP	Poverty Reduction Strategy Paper
PSA	Production Sharing Agreement
PWYP	Publish What You Pay
REDD	Reducing Emissions from Deforestation and Forest Degradation in Developing Countries
RWI	Revenue Watch Institute
SADC	Southern African Development Community
SEA	Strategic Environmental Assessment
TWN	Third World Network
UK	United Kingdom
UN	United Nations
UNCTAD	United Nations Conference on Trade and Development
UNEP	United Nations Environment Programme
UNGA	United Nations General Assembly
UNOSAA	United Nations Office of the Special Adviser on Africa
UNU-INRA	United Nations University-Institute for Natural Resources in Africa
USA	United States of America
USD	United States dollars

WBG	World Bank Group
WCED	World Commission on Environment and Development

Chapter One

Collaborative Governance and its Relevance for Extractive Industries in Africa

Timothy Afful-Koomson[1]

Introduction

In the past 20 years, Africa has seen numerous conflict escalations, some with deadly consequences, which relate to the development and management of extractive resources on the continent. Conflicts in petroleum- and mineral-rich African countries often have to do with access to, or distribution and allocation of, revenues from extractive industries. The links between conflicts and extractive resources have led to increased interest in and the exploration of public policy systems and structures that could create a forum where the divergent and entrenched interests and positions of the various stakeholders could be addressed without any of them resorting to deadly conflicts. There is also the need to find effective ways of dealing with negative environmental impacts of the operations, corruption, and mismanagement of revenues from extractive resources. The intent is to ensure that these revenues are used for national development that is sustainable, diversified and socially inclusive. Such national development would provide alternative forms of economic activities, employment, incomes and also improved living conditions, particularly for communities affected by the operations of extractive industries.

The first substantive response to these challenges confronting the extractive industries came from the World Bank Group (WBG). It was primarily the result of intense criticisms from the non-governmental community of the WBG's support, both financial

---

[1] Senior Research Fellow, Environmental Policy, United Nations University - Institute for Natural Resources in Africa

1

and technical, for the extraction of resources, which had a host of negative consequences, including environmental degradation and mismanagement of resource revenues that could fuel conflicts. At an annual meeting in Prague, Czech Republic, in June 2000, then World Bank President James Wolfensohn, responded to this criticism by promising to review the WBG role in the extractive sector. This response then led to the Extractive Industries Review (EIR) report in 2003. The EIR is currently institutionalised with an advisory group, meetings, annual reporting and monitoring on progress made and challenges confronting the implementation of the EIR recommendations.

Of particular relevance to the focus of this book are the three main enabling conditions proposed by the EIR. These are: (1) pro-poor public and corporate governance, including proactive planning and management to maximise poverty alleviation through sustainable development; (2) effective social and environmental policies, and; (3) respect for human rights. On governance, the EIR recommended criteria that emphasise transparency and the broad involvement of all stakeholders. The minimum core and sectorial governance criteria should embrace "the quality of the rule of law, the absence of armed conflicts or of a high risk of such conflict, respect for labour standards and human rights, recognition of and willingness to protect the rights of indigenous peoples; and government capacity to promote sustainable development through economic diversification" (EIR, 2003:2).

In June 2006, the United Nations Office of the Special Adviser on Africa (UNOSAA) followed up on the EIR by organising an expert group meeting in collaboration with the Government of Egypt on '*Natural Resources and Conflict in Africa: Transforming a Peace Liability into a Peace Asset*'. The meeting focused on improving natural resource governance with a particular emphasis on ways that wealth from extracted resources could be transformed from being major triggers of conflicts into engines for durable peace and sustainable development in Africa (UNOSAA, 2006). One of the outcomes of this meeting that is pertinent to the focus of this book is the recommendation to treat issues involving extractive natural resources development as governance issues, which should be addressed at all levels. Governance issues include: political governance that should be participatory, transparent and accountable; economic governance that embraces efficient and effective economic management including systems of revenue and expenditure management, and; corporate governance with government regulatory structures and corporate social responsibility (UNOSAA, 2006).

The United Nations (UN) has also advanced its commitment towards improved governance of extractive industries with the Resolution on the Extractive Industries Transparency Initiative (EITI) that was adopted at the 62nd session of the UN General Assembly. The Resolution makes provision for voluntary initiatives, such as EITI, to "ensure transparency and verifiable processes, while adhering to and promoting the principles of honesty, transparency and accountability in order to maximise the contribution of the private sector to the realisation of social and people-centred sustainable development" (UNGA, 2008:4).

At the regional level, there are several ad hoc initiatives and high-level declarations intended to promote sustainable development of extractive resources in Africa. However, there is no specific and substantive initiative similar to the EIR that deals exclusively with extractive industries on the continent. The African Union Convention on Combating and Preventing Corruption and the African Peer Review Mechanism (APRM), both established in 2003 (NEPAD, 2012), are probably seen to be serving as the instruments that will also help governance of extractive industries. The APRM in particular comprises four focal areas dealing with governance:

1) democracy and good political governance that ensures the constitutions of member states reflect democratic ethos, accountable governance and promotion of political representation in a free and fair political environment;
2) good economic governance that focuses on transparency in financial management as an essential pre-requisite for promoting economic growth and poverty reduction;
3) corporate governance that supports the promotion of ethical principles, values and practices that are in line with broader social and economic goals benefiting all citizens, and;
4) socio-economic development that focuses on poverty reduction through the promotion of democracy, good

3

governance, peace and security, as well as the development of human and physical resources (NEPAD, 2012).

The APRM is a welcome initiative that could serve as the framework for country-specific structures, components and requirements for effective governance of the extractive industries in Africa. However, it is a voluntary instrument, with no operational tools and indicators for assessing performance. The self-assessment and monitoring process may compromise its usefulness as an effective governance mechanism.

Some key issues that are central to the recommendations of the EIR, the UNOSAA initiative and the APRM and consistent across the board are that the appropriate governance regime should be transparent and accountable, with broader avenues for participation by all stakeholders, including indigenous people. It should have a pro-poor agenda in promoting economic growth and poverty reduction while respecting labour standards, human rights, ethical and environmental principles, values and practices. The appropriate governance regime should also be buttressed by effective democratic and constitutional principles, respect for the rule of law, peace and security.

A survey of financial assistance for activities related to governance of extractive industries in Africa estimated about US$230 million for 61 projects in Africa from 2004-2006. About 70 percent of the financial assistance was provided by the World Bank for activities including capacity development, policy dialogue and institutional support. The report on this survey emphasises quality of governance as a key factor influencing the ability of countries to use revenues from their extractive industries for development (AfDB, 2007). According to the report of the Africa Progress Panel that is chaired by Kofi Annan - former Secretary-General of the UN, "Africa has never suffered from a "resource curse". What the region has suffered from is the curse of poor policies, weak governance and a failure to translate resource wealth into social and economic progress" (APP, 2013:22).

The major focus of this chapter is to explore the appropriate governance regime with the key structures, components and features that could encompass some of the critical issues raised above. In line with this focus, the chapter will discuss the relevance of a collaborative governance regime for extractive industries in Africa. It provides a brief overview of collaborative governance by looking at what it is (definitions and descriptions), what it involves (basic elements, features, components or constituents) and why it is of value to governing and managing extractive industries in Africa (its usefulness, functionality and also limitations).

The intent is not to present an elaborate model of collaborative governance. Rather, it is to explore how collaborative governance could serve as the framework for a regime capable of addressing the critical issues, including transparency, accountability, and broader stakeholder participation in a contentious policy environment, such as that involving extractive industries. The discussion is guided by the characteristics of extractive industries, such as diverse and sometimes conflicting interests, demands, positions, and group dynamics, as well as the contentious area of resource revenues and the disputes they engender. The author is aware of the diversity within the extractive sector, which includes mining for diverse minerals as well as the extraction of petroleum resources, and of the many differences in national legal and policy environments. There are also specific conditions, contexts and settings that may limit the broader application of this framework as a generic and all-inclusive framework for governing and managing the extractive industries. However, there could be selective applications of particular elements or components of a collaborative governance regime that may be appropriate for a particular nation, sector, and settings.

What is governance?

Because one of the critical components of collaborative governance is the meaning of governance itself, it is essential to start with a clear understanding of that term and how it is used in this book. There is currently no conceptually comprehensive and widely accepted theory of governance. Governance has been used to describe many political processes, institutions, decision-making and management entities. The term has been used to imply the minimal state, new public management, the socio-cybernetic system, self-organising networks, policy-making in the absence of an overarching political authority, withdrawal of the European

5

welfare state and even public sector reforms in Africa (Rhodes, 1996, Krahmann, 2003).

There are different and distinct types of governance, including social, political, corporate and environmental. Although the diverse usage of the term gives it a broad range of usefulness, the ambiguities involving its wide-ranging application and sometimes conflicting conceptualisation may constrain the development of a conceptually coherent theory of governance. Its diverse usage has also resulted in several definitions of governance. As a result, definitions of governance are as varied as the issues and levels of analysis to which the concept is applied (Krahmann, 2003). Most of the definitions thus have limited usage and may be comprehensibly applicable only in the discipline or sphere of practice of the original author that is credited with a particular definition. This book focuses on governance as a mechanism of public policy.

According to Leach et al. (2007), governance can be defined in a broader sense to refer to political processes and institutions, which are its two key components. Through these political processes and institutions, governance "shapes how scientific and technological processes are directed, how environmental and health issues are defined and addressed, and how social consequences are distributed. They shape and are shaped by the interactions between people, technology and environment, and how these dynamics unfold over time" (Leach et al., 2007:1). Thus institutions form the fundamental structures for decision-making on a wide range of development issues. They are also the mechanisms for the allocation of power, which usually determines who gets what - and also what percentage of the national goods and services one receives. The competition for control over resource allocation and distribution underpins the transformation of governance as decision-making processes into political processes, in which the divergent interests, positions, demands and expectations of the different institutions clash (Afful-Koomson, 2012). There are few public policy arenas where this transformation of governance is more applicable than the policy arena of extractive industries.

According to O'Toole (2000), governance involves a "multi-layered structural context of rule-governed understanding, along with the role of multiple social actors in arrays of negotiation, implementation and service delivery. Addressing governance requires attending to social patterns and ideas about how to concert action among them". Implicit in this definition is the expectation that realising the outcome of concerted action for policy- and decision-making involves complex negotiations, positioning, bargaining, trade-offs and other exchanges among the key actors. The interactions and exchanges are likely to produce consensus and broad ownership of negotiated agreements when the power relationships between the actors are symmetrical; there are more flexibility and gestures of compromise between actors on a fairly level playing field. When the relationship is asymmetrical and power is concentrated in the hands of one or a few actors with the clout to dominate and impose their interests and demands on the other equally legitimate actors, the furtherance of concerted actions becomes very remote (Afful-Koomson, 2012). There is a good deal of evidence that when it comes to extractive industries, 'powerless' stakeholders have opted for armed conflicts as a countervailing form of power because of the asymmetry of power allocation in the public decision-making system.

Theoretical building blocks of governance

In the absence of a coherent and comprehensive theory of governance, Afful-Koomson (2012) recommends the use of theoretical building blocks of governance. The intent is to provide key epistemic panels that could help construct a fairly lucid theoretical framework to enhance understanding of what governance is. The five key theoretical building blocks of governance are discussed below.

Governance involves 'hollowing' out of the state and its legitimate powers

It is argued that the traditional concepts of the state having the monopoly over the legitimate use of decision-making authority, and of government as the sole entity that controls the distribution of power and resources of a nation, are outmoded (Bekke et al., 1995, Peters and Pierre, 1998). Unlike government, governance involves a 'hollowing out' of the state by distributing power to other key actors (Rhodes, 1997, Peters and Pierre, 1998). Some of

7

the noted examples for this hollowing out the legitimate powers of the state include public activities that are delegated to non-state agencies at the national and local levels, or when the state relinquishes to multilateral institutions its sovereign jurisdiction over national issues or resources with global or trans-boundary dimensions (Rhodes, 1997, Leach et al., 2007). This is particularly relevant when, within the frame of contractual agreements, a state cedes to multinational companies the control over the exploitation, allocation and distribution of national goods and services. This argument may have some conceptual traction considering the current age of globalisation where the territorial range of authority that defines the classical state is more diffused. This is also the age where multinational companies, especially those with interests in the extractive sector in the developing world, are assuming greater roles in defining the levels of development and distribution of wealth from and within countries. Bribery, corporate corrupt practices and perpetuation of political corruption by some extractive companies in Africa all compromise the legitimacy of a governance model that involves the hollowing out of the state by according ever-more clout to corporate entities.

Although hollowing out may be viewed by some scholars as tantamount to a decline in state powers (Rhodes, 1997, Peters and Pierre, 1998, Stoker, 2000) and in the centrality of the state (Leach et al., 2007), there may also be advantages if the state *strategically* hollows out its decision-making and policy implementation authority by devolving it to competent non-state actors. This could enable the state to leverage the expertise, resources and capacities of non-state actors to complement what are often scarce resources, low capacity and limited expertise of the state. When the state itself strategically initiates the hollowing out, not to entrench the locus and scope of its traditional bureaucratic and political authority, but to tap into the competencies of other stakeholders, it may actually expand its development capacities. It may also improve the availability of resources and capacity for effective policies and efficient delivery of national goods and services. Moreover, when the state strategically hollows out its powers to competent stakeholders, it explicitly recognises and legitimises the value of their collaboration. This strategic and concerted alliance may transform the image of the state from being authoritarian to being a catalyst, facilitator, adviser and coordinator for national development (Afful-Koomson, 2012). Authoritarian regimes have been linked with a greater tendency for political corruption and mismanagement of extractive resources and revenues, as demonstrated by Amundsen in Chapter 7 of this book. Transforming the image of most authoritarian governments in Africa by genuinely hollowing out powers to competent stakeholders can improve transparency and accountability in the management of revenues from extractive industries and in turn engender remarkable outcomes in sustainable development on the continent.

Governance involves making state officials and organisations effective and efficient.

This second conceptual building block of governance draws largely from analytical models of the new public management (NPM) movement. According to Peters and Pierre (1998), governance and NPM have a common feature in terms of their changing views of the roles of elected officials. Both NPM and governance models undervalue the classic Weberian view of political officers as elites wielding the power of domination, legitimisation and authority. Both also recognise that the traditional roles that should be reserved for political officers are those needed for defining and setting the goals and priorities of the public sector. Peters and Pierre (1998) therefore support a governance model in which elected officials are political entrepreneurs whose role is to facilitate the development of networks and to pool public and private resources.

For public organisations, it is argued that their highly centralised and hierarchical structure make them inefficient and ineffective in the delivery of public goods and services (Rhodes, 1997, Peters and Pierre, 1998, Stoker, 2000). One strand of the argument advocates pruning the Weberian bureaucratic structure of all unnecessary power appendages and branches to make it leaner, more diversified, integrated and efficient (Peters and Pierre, 1998). Another strand of the argument proposes the introduction of corporate mechanisms, such as competitive tendering, internal auditing, performance indicators and incentives, to make public organisations more efficient, accountable and transparent (Peters and Pierre, 1998, Krahmann, 2003). These mechanisms are highly

9

relevant for transparency of concessions and contracts for extractive industries and for accountability in the management of the resource revenues that accrue from them.

Governance involves the active participation of private actors in policy-making and implementation.

Governance has also been distinguished from government by describing the emergence of policy-making arrangements that increasingly involve private actors such as non-governmental agencies, firms, associations and interest groups in the provision of public services and in social and economic regulation (Krahmann, 2003). According to Stoker (2000) 'governance refers to the development of governing styles in which the boundaries between and within public and private sectors have become blurred. The essence of governance is its focus on mechanisms that do not rest on recourse to the authority and sanctions of government'. Governance facilitates the involvement of private actors by providing the potential for contracting, franchising and instituting new forms of regulations (Stoker, 2000), and by providing the avenue of participation in the provision of public services through privatisation, outsourcing, co-production and public-private partnerships (PPPs) (Krahmann, 2003). By providing the avenue for constructive participation of non-state actors, governance could provide public organisations with diverse and multiple instruments for policy-making and their implementation in the extractive industries. According to Peters and Pierre (1998), when a government enters into a PPP for policy, it indicates its willingness to operate within the governance framework to develop alternative means of making and implementing policy. Providing the avenue for active participation by private actors demonstrates a government's flexibility and willingness to innovate in the selection of policy instruments. Governance may therefore imply the use of a wider repertoire of instruments than might be used by a more traditional public sector (Peters and Pierre, 1998), and it may also involve coordinated efforts and interactions between diverse actors, institutions and artefacts (Leach et al., 2007).

Governance involves the mutual reinforcement of the potentials of public policy and markets.

A related notion of improving the efficiency of public organisations and of promoting private actors' participation in policy-making as conceptual building blocks of governance is the relationship between public policy and markets within a neo-Keynesian economic framework. Leach et al. (2007), drawing from Scharpf (1997), reiterate that the emergence of governance perspectives does not signal the demise of public institutions or of markets. Rather, governance provides the frame for blurring the respective potentials of these two long-established institutions (Rhodes, 1997, Leach et al., 2007). The operation of internal markets is critical for competition within public organisations (Peters and Pierre, 1998). It may also ensure cost-effectiveness, comparative performance analysis and benchmarking, and improve customer service, accountability and efficiency. This reiterates the recommendation by the UNOSAA (2006) for economic governance that involves efficient and effective management of expenditures on and revenues from extractive industries.

However, it is worth noting that despite their instrumentality in ensuring efficiency, relying too heavily on markets could also constrain the range of choice available to a nation. They could serve as potential sources of resource waste and may induce institutions to over-supply services (March and Olsen, 1989, Whitley and Kristensen, 1997, Peters and Pierre, 1998). This is the case with the link between price performance in the commodity market and the level of exploitation and export of unprocessed or under processed extractive products from Africa.

Governance involves the use of networks and partnerships for collective action.

"Perhaps the dominant feature of the governance model is the argument that networks have come to dominate public policy" (Peters and Pierre 1998, 225). Although usually considered as unstructured, the flexibility, dynamism and transient nature of networks provide them with sufficient resilience and capacity for self-organisation (Marsh and Rhodes, 1992, Peters and Pierre, 1998). These features have made networks emerge as preferred modes of steering and coordination for realising policy objectives

(Stoker, 2000, Leach et al., 2007). Networks and partnerships are also becoming more important as an alternative to the hierarchical and centralised system of government because their structure is more horizontally integrated and there is no single member in the network or partnership that has the monopoly on decision-making authority. Government institutions participate in the networks as equals and they are mutually dependent on the other non-state actors to the same extent as the other actors are dependent on them. This however, does not make the state totally impotent. Rather, its role and capacity evolve from direct control to influence and the state now has to bargain with the other stakeholders in the network as relative equals rather than resorting to unilateral use of power if it deems decisions and outcomes are not favourable (Peters and Pierre, 1998).

The use of networks facilitates the blending of public and private sector resources and, when done within formal partnership agreements, this may permit public and private partners to have access to resources and capacities that might not be at their disposal outside the realm of the partnership. Rhodes (1988) and Peters and Pierre (1998) note that previously this mutual resource dependency has been associated largely with the relationship between central governments and sub-national government institutions but that it has been extended in the current context to cover the 'gamut of relationships' between central government and the other organisations with which it interacts.

The issues, interests and positions characterising the policy arena of extractive industries are complex and diverse, requiring an alliance of stakeholders that not only share common and collective interests but also possess diverse resources and capabilities for collective action. The cooperation among stakeholders in the network, alliance or partnership is premised on a relationship of equals and the achievement of collective action that does not rest on recourse to the authority of the state (Stoker, 2000, Richards and Smith, 2002). There are intricate interdependencies among stakeholders of the network and their pursuit of collective actions enhances the synergies between them.

Some scholars are of the opinion that the significance of knowledge in the conceptualisation of society-nature interactions (such as the use of natural resources) should make this knowledge an important dimension of governance and an important component in contemporary mainstream thinking and practice in governance (Melucci, 1995, Fischer, 2003, Leach et al., 2007). When knowledge is conceptualised in this context, it could be perceived as part of the resources and capacities that are brought into the network or partnership by some of the network stakeholders. This conceptualisation is particularly useful for governance of the extractive industries. Knowledge is power, and recognising the importance of the non-formal indigenous knowledge of local communities affected by the operations of extractive industries will legitimise their participation in the governance network. We can now talk about different dimensions of power - political, knowledge, investment and technological - in a complementarity of the networks.

In summary, governance is about institutions, actors, networks and the political processes that define policy- and decision-making to advance a particular development path. It involves 'hollowing out' or distributing power from the state to other competent private stakeholders to enable them to participate actively in policy-making and implementation. It also involves: making state officials and organisations effective and efficient; encouraging the active participation of private actors in policy-making and implementation; providing the setting for the mutual reinforcement of the potentials of public policy and markets, and; using networks and partnerships for collective action.

What is collaborative governance?

The two key words here are collaborative and governance. It is hoped that the theoretical building blocks of governance discussed above will facilitate the understanding of what governance is. In the following sections, this chapter will provide the definitions and key features that distinguish collaborative governance from other forms of governance. Ansell and Gash (2007:544) define collaborative governance as " a governing arrangement where one or more public agencies directly engage non-state stakeholders in a collective decision-making process that is formal, consensus-oriented, and deliberative and that aims to make or implement public policy or manage public programmes or assets". According to Emerson et al. (2011:2) collaborative governance can be defined

13

"broadly as the processes and structures of public policy decision-making and management that engage people constructively across the boundaries of public agencies, levels of government, and/or the public, private and civic spheres in order to carry out a public purpose that could not otherwise be accomplished".

According to Ansell and Gash (2007), some of the terms used interchangeably with collaborative governance include 'participatory management', 'interactive policy-making', 'stakeholder governance' and 'collaborative management'. Fung (2002) use the term 'participatory collaboration'. Ansell and Gash (2007) clarify some of the confusion about the use of synonyms of collaborative governance. Examples are: 'corporatism' that may apply tripartite bargaining process similar to collaborative governance but may lack broader participation by all stakeholders with representational monopoly over their sectors or groups. Another is the 'public-private partnership' that may imply joint efforts by public and private actors for implementing tasks and service delivery, in which collective decision-making may be secondary to the performance of the joint activities and not formalised in the process. Like collaborative governance, 'policy networking' may also involve public agencies and non-state stakeholders and use cooperative modes of decision-making, but it may operate through informal multilateral processes such as shuttle diplomacy. As discussed below, one of the key features of a collaborative governance regime is that the multilateral processes are formalised and institutionalised.

What are the key features of collaborative governance?

Definitions may hide key features of a theory that may limit its empirical utility. This section will therefore provide and examine some of the key features of collaborative governance.

The term 'collaborative governance' has been used by scientists and practitioners of public policy to refer to a new form of governance that has been emerging to replace more top-down adversarial governance and managerial modes of policy-making and implementation (Fung, 2002, Ansell and Gash, 2007). According to Fung (2002:8), collaborative governance "focuses on public problem-solving, is partially decentralised, invites citizen participation and occurs in a continuous and institutionalised way". Ansell and Gash (2007) provide six criteria for collaborative governance, four of which are consistent with the features provided by Fung (2002). They include: the focus is on public policy or public management (public problem-solving); the forum is formally organised and meets collectively (continuous and institutionalised), and; participants include non-state actors (citizen participation). The other criteria are: participants engage directly in decision-making and are not merely 'consulted' by public agencies; the forum aims to make decisions by consensus (even if consensus is not achieved in practice), and; the forum is initiated by public agencies. The latter criterion is problematic because it limits collaborative governance to only state-initiated arrangements (Emerson et al., 2011). Moreover, consensus as an outcome of collective decision-making may be a value of collaborative governance and not necessarily a feature, so that will be addressed in the next section.

The five main features discussed in this section have been selected on the basis of their relevance in collaborative governance and management of extractive industries in Africa. They are:

- broader representation by all stakeholders;
- formalised and institutionalised collaboration;
- focus on public policy,
- multilateral and collective decision-making
- decentralised process of problem-solving.

1. A key feature that underpins collaborative governance is that it should provide broader avenues for representation and participation by private stakeholders. Without the representation and participation of non-state actors, the term can be reduced to 'collaborative government', which is distinct from collaborative governance. The earlier section on key theoretical building blocks of governance emphasises this feature. Emerson et al., (2011), citing Mill ('Considerations on Representative Government,' 1861, p. 35), notes that, 'the quality of governance arrangements should be judged first by the extent to which they foster good and capable citizens and second according to the degree to which they utilise these abilities to advance good public ends'. The emphasis is therefore on active participation and not just mere representation.

15

This is why non-state actors (particularly community stakeholders) in extractive industries should be provided with the capacity, skills and information they need to make their diverse resources, and with knowledge and capabilities of value to the collaborative governance process. If participating community stakeholders do not understand accounting principles, budgeting, revenue and expenditure management, their participation in collaborative governance can have little or no value for improving financial transparency and accountability in extractive industries.

2. There is one feature that distinguishes collaborative governance from other forms of collaboration, such as local business and community group collaboration (Fung, 2002) and policy networks and agency-interest group governance (Ansell and Gash, 2007), namely that the interactions among the stakeholders are formalised and institutionalised. This involves strategic and concerted initiatives to establish structure and organisation for the interactions and activities (Ansell and Gash, 2007). It also "requires concrete changes in the formal procedures of public agencies, reallocation of public authority across levels of government and lines separating government from governed, and shifts in the roles of officials, interest organisations, and citizens themselves" (Fung, 2002:10). Although imposing the requirement for institutionalised and formalised settings for collaborative governance may limit its application (Emerson et al., 2011), this may be the critical requirement for improving legitimacy, transparency and accountability in extractive industries. Currently, there are different levels of interactions and arrangements among public agencies, extractive companies and local communities in most mineral-rich countries in Africa. However, because these interactions are not formalised and institutionalised and many of the initiatives are undertaken with ad hoc arrangements, extractive industries in Africa are still characterised by persistent adversarial situations, sabotages and deadly conflicts, as shown in many chapters in this book (Darimani, for example, discusses some of these informal governance arrangements in Chapter 4).

3. Collaborative governance focuses on solving problems in the public and not the private sphere. While acknowledging the ambiguity of the boundary between public and private issues, Ansell and Gash (2007) stress that one distinguishing feature of

collaborative governance is its focus on public policies and issues. According to Fung (2002), when stakeholders of a collaborative governance regime work together to formulate mutually agreed plans, implement policies and embed lasting rules in public law, they do so to address common concerns and not to serve their own interests. The focus on public policies and issues is not meant to place decision-making and implementation relating to these issues in the exclusive domain of public stakeholders. In a collaborative governance regime, public stakeholders are "neither neutral arbiters nor sole implementers. They convene other citizens and groups, but often participate in substantive policy development and join with private parties in the implementation of public decisions" (Fung, 2002:8).

4. As noted in the section above on the building blocks of governance, governance involves consultation with and participation of non-state stakeholders. However, there are several levels of consultation and participation. These range from merely informing the non-state stakeholders about the decisions made and the related mechanisms for their implementation, to soliciting feedback or advice from them without their active involvement in the decision-making and implementation, to the active participation of non-state stakeholders with commitment to and ownership of the decision-making and implementation processes. Of these, the latter is the level required for collaborative governance. For example, Ansell and Gash (2007) impose the condition of direct engagement of non-state stakeholders through intense communication and multilateral deliberation to formulate and implement decisions of common interests. Non-state stakeholders should also have responsibility for policy outcomes.

5. Collaborative governance should also have a decentralised setting for problem-solving. Fung (2002) recognise the feasibility of decentralised regulatory processes and the establishment of procedures and conditions for decentralised problem-solving. He proposes, however, that the process involving the development of solutions be devolved to the local stakeholders, so that it benefits from the diversity of information and knowledge they possess. The governance and management of extractive industries are highly contentious, so local knowledge and information are not only critical for local implementation but should also be incorporated in

the formulation of the policies, regulations and decisions. Decentralised problem-solving should not be limited to involving local or district branches of government institutions. According to Afful-Koomson (2012), when decentralised problem-solving is conceived and applied this way, the district and local branches of government institutions merely become the conduits for extending government bureaucratic influence and operations to the local level. Decentralised problem-solving should rather involve the empowerment of local independent networks, agencies and organisations that can participate as active partners with local branches of government institutions to develop collective actions to solve issues of common interests.

What is the value of collaborative governance for extractive industries in Africa?

Extractive industries in Africa have been associated with conflicts that have arisen over the control, distribution and utilisation of the resources and revenues from extractive operations. These resource and revenue conflicts have resulted in unfortunate rent-seeking strategies, bribery, corruption, and the misuse of public monies. As demonstrated throughout this book, these practices are going on amidst increasing environmental degradation, unemployment and worsening poverty, particularly in communities where these extractive resources are exploited. One of the reasons for these 'ills' afflicting the operations of so many extractive industries in Africa is the top-down, 'opaque,' adversarial and dysfunctional system governing and managing them. Collaborative governance has the potential to contribute to collective and consensus-oriented decision-making in extractive industries. It also has the potential to improve transparency and accountability in revenue management for inclusive growth and sustainable development of resource-rich countries in Africa.

It is appropriate to acknowledge that collaborative governance has some shortcomings and may not be the absolute panacea for all the 'ills' of most extractive industries in Africa. These may include "the erosion of state authority, administrative incompetence, apathy and absence of citizen participation, and local political inequality and domination" (Fung, 2002:3). Collaborative governance can also be a very demanding process, both time-consuming and with uncertain outcomes (Fung, 2002, Ansell and Gash, 2007). It may not be effective if commitment is lacking, or if the process is 'hijacked' by some stakeholders and used to manipulate others. It could also create persistent distrust among stakeholders (Fung and Wright, 2001, Huxham and Vangen, 2004, Ansell and Gash, 2007, and Johnston et al., 2010).

Notwithstanding these shortcomings, a collaborative governance regime has some pertinent structures and functionalities that may offer possibilities for finding solutions to some of the complex and intractable issues affecting most extractive industries in Africa. Some of the potential benefits of collaborative governance include 'innovation in the methods of public problem-solving, greater reach and subtlety of public action, information advantages, legitimacy, equity, public deliberation and civic education' (Fung, 2002). The specific usefulness of collaborative governance to extractive industries may also include the decline in current adversarial policy and decision-making, and improved consensus and collective action for problem-solving. It can also enhance transparency and accountability in decision-making and in revenue management.

Chapters in this book

It is appropriate to briefly discuss here the background for this book and the various chapters. The core activities of the United Nations University – Institute for Natural Resources in Africa (UNU-INRA) are research, capacity development and policy support that enhance sustainable development and management of the continent's natural resources. This involves the pursuit of its commitment to contribute to regional initiatives that improve governance of the extractive industries in Africa, and UNU-INRA has devoted an entire programme specifically to this issue. 'Governing and Managing the Extractive Industries' is one of the three programme areas of the UNU-INRA Strategic Plan 2011–2014. One of the objectives of this programme area is to explore the governance regime for the extractive sector in Africa. This includes the identification and examination of the key structures, components and features that could address the critical issues facing extractive industries. This quest led to the consideration of a collaborative governance regime.

19

As a follow-up to this process, UNU-INRA organised the *International Conference on Sustainable Development of Natural Resources in Africa (ICSDNRA 2011) in Accra, Ghana, from December 5 to 7, 2011.* The theme for the second day of the conference was *'Enhancing Collaborative Governance and Management of the Extractive Industries for Equitable Wealth Distribution and Environmental Management in Africa'.* UNU-INRA was able to assemble from across Africa representatives from government, extractive companies, traditional institutions and leaders (such as chiefs and queens), academia and civil society organisations to deliberate and recommend solutions to these critical issues.

With the exception of chapters 7 and 8, all the chapters in this book were selected from presentations at the ICSDNRA 2011. The issues addressed by these are presented in the contexts of the different countries, sectors and settings in which they were documented and analysed. However, they all illustrate some common characteristics of extractive industries, including resource conflicts, and divergent stakeholders' interests, needs and positions. They also demonstrate the dysfunctional, state-dominated policy-making systems that entrench corruption and the mismanagement of revenue from extractive resources and that externalise the negative environmental impacts of the operations of extractive companies.

This introductory chapter has focused on some of the related definitions and features characterising the theory and practice of collaborative governance regimes. It also examined how useful a collaborative governance regime can be in improving governance and management of extractive industries in Africa.

In the second chapter, Kwadwo Tutu from the Economics Department of the University of Ghana, discusses ways of improving the management of mineral resources for sustainable development in Africa. He looks at the lingering paradox of Africa as a continent rich in natural resources and yet afflicted by extreme poverty, and also the worsening conflicts and environmental degradation related to natural resource extraction. He examines the current state of mineral resource exploitation in Africa and the proper role that the mineral wealth should play in addressing the three key pillars of sustainable development (economic, social and environment) on the continent. He also discusses inter-generational equity issues and how these should guide the equitable distribution of wealth from mineral resources and the role of mining companies in conflict resolution and sustainable development.

In Chapter 3, Madonna Dolphyne from Centralian Consulting Foundation briefly reviews the 'resource curse' hypothesis and she analyses its implications for development in mineral-rich countries in Africa. Her premise is that mineral endowments are a form of implicit capital with the potential to spur socio-economic growth. To realise these, however, she argues that there are critical challenges, such as distribution and management of resource revenues, which must be addressed appropriately and this mineral wealth should be invested in infrastructure, facilities and services that improve the living standards of the citizens. She discusses the conditions, success factors and strategies that can maximise the contribution of the mineral sector to growth and development in Africa. She also examines some policy options and strategies that may help promote growth and reduce poverty, particularly in mining communities.

Chapter 4 examines governance in the Ghanaian mining sector. Abdulai Darimani, of Third World Network – Africa, a research and advocacy organisation based in Accra, Ghana, takes a qualitative approach in his analysis, integrating data from participant observations at relevant meetings and conferences with information from a review of secondary materials. He illustrates how governance can work for actors and the environment in mining communities in Ghana and assesses the role of governance in the distribution of mineral wealth and in the management of environmental risks. He concludes from the analysis that governance in the study area has produced some important outputs. However, it has not contributed to any change in the asymmetry of power and the disproportionate distribution of benefits and environmental burdens in the mining sector. He provides some recommendations for enhancing governance in mining communities.

In Chapter 5, Frank K. Nyame from the Department of Earth Science, University of Ghana, discusses labour specialisation and sustenance of artisanal small-scale mining (ASM) in Ghana. Based on data from several mining communities in Ghana, he examines

21

the significant transformations in ASM towards distinct differentiation or 'specialisation' beyond the usual gender- and/or age-based categorisations. He maintains that the 'specialised or semi-specialised' labour and services are helping to sustain the bourgeoning artisanal mining activities in mineral-rich areas of the country and probably also throughout the West African sub-region. He also looks at the impacts of the labour specialisation on socio-economic development and environmental management in mining communities.

Chapter 6 brings non-African experiences and perspectives from studies in small- and medium-scale mining in Guyana, South America. Paulette Bynoe from the University of Guyana examines the socio-economic benefits and environmental impacts of the small- and medium-scale gold mining sector in Guyana. She discusses the effectiveness of past and current environmental governance mechanisms, including Guyana's low carbon development strategies, in addressing several issues and concerns of Guyanese stakeholders. She draws out lessons that could be contextualised and replicated in Africa and also recommends how socio-economic and environmental management issues in the mining sector could be aligned with a low carbon development strategy.

Chapter 7 marks a transition from the focus on governance and management issues involving mining activities to those of oil and gas extraction. Inge Amundsen from the Chr. Michelsen Institute in Norway discusses the challenges of improving management of petroleum revenue in Africa. He reviews the 'resource curse' hypothesis (discussed in Chapter 3 in reference to the mining sector) and how it relates to institutions and corruption involving revenues from petroleum resources development in Africa. He dissects the institutional challenges and examines them as two main facets of resource extraction and revenue redistribution. He also analyses the dynamics of collusion, power brokerage, mutual empowerment and entrenchment in the control and mismanagement of petroleum revenues. He takes a deeper look at pervasive corrupt practices in some petroleum-exporting countries in Africa and how measures to improve transparency, accountability, and efficiency in petroleum revenue management will help Ghana avoid joining the 'team' of corrupt oil-producing nations on the continent.

In Chapter 8, Joe Asamoah of EnerWise Africa, a consulting, research and development company, presents a comprehensive analysis of the oil find in Ghana with some historical and technical information. He also references the 'resource curse' hypothesis and the related 'Dutch Disease' that affects most petroleum-exporting countries in Africa. He stresses the urgent need to enhance the capacity of relevant institutions such as the Ghana National Petroleum Corporation (GNPC) to help improve efficiency and accountability in development and management of petroleum products and revenues in Ghana. He also advises in light of the high expectations of Ghanaians as a result of the oil find and offers some measures that could maximise the benefits from petroleum development for inclusive growth in Ghana.

In Chapter 9, Timothy Afful-Koomson summarises the key issues and findings in the book and discusses how collaborative governance could be applied to improve equitable wealth distribution of revenues from extractive industries in Africa and also to reduce their environmental impacts on local communities. He also provides some critical considerations that should guide the design of the collaboration governance regime, its process, the dynamics and implementation of governance matters, and how to manage the related outcomes.

References

AfDB, 2007. Governance of the extractive industries in Africa: Survey of donor-funded assistance. African Development Bank in collaboration with NORAD and the World Bank. Abidjan: African Development Bank.

Afful-Koomson, T. 2012. Governance challenges for promoting the green economy in Africa. In: DE Oliveira, J. A. P. (ed.) Green economy and good governance for sustainable development: Opportunities, promises and concerns. Tokyo: United Nations University Press.

Ansell, C. and Gash, A. 2007. Collaborative governance in theory and practice. Journal of Public Administration Research and Theory 18, 543–571.

APP. 2013. Equity in extractives: Stewarding Africa's natural resources for all. Geneva: Africa Progress Report 2013.

Bekke, H., Kickert, W. J. M. and Kooiman, J. 1995. Public management governance in public policy and administrative sciences in The Netherlands. London: Harvester-Wheatsheaf.

EIR. 2003. Striking a better balance: The extractive industries review [Online]. Jakarta/Washington, DC: World Bank Group and Extractive Industries. http://go.worldbank.org/T1VB5JCV61 [Accessed 4 September 2012].

Emerson, K., Nabatchi, K. and Balogh, S. 2011. An integrative framework of collaborative governance. Journal of Public Administration Research and Theory 22, 1 –29.

Fischer, F. 2003. Reframing public policy: Discursive politics and deliberative practices. Oxford: Oxford University Press.

Fung, A. 2002. Collaboration and countervailing power: Making participatory governance work. www.archonfung.net/papers/CollaborativePower2.2.pdf [Accessed 22 August 2012].

Fung, A. and Wright, E. O. 2001. Deepening democracy: Innovations in empowered participatory governance. Politics and Society 29, 5–41.

Huxham, C. and Vangen, S. 2004. Doing things collaboratively: Realising the advantage or succumbing to inertia. organisational dynamics 33, 190–201.

Johnston, E. W., Hicks, D., Nan, N. and Auer, J. C. 2010. Managing the inclusion process in collaborative governance. Journal of Public Administration Research and Theory 21, 699–721.

Krahmann, E. 2003. National, regional and global governance: One phenomenon of many? Global Governance 9: 323–346.

Leach, M., Bloom, G., Ely, A., Nightingale, P., Scoones, I., Shah, E. and Smith, A. 2007. Understanding governance: Pathways to sustainability. Brighton: STEPS Centre, University of Sussex.

March, J. G. and Olsen, J. P. 1989. Rediscovering institutions, New York: Free Press.

Marsh, D. and Rhodes, R. 1992. Policy networks in British government. Oxford: Clarendon Press.

Melucci, A. 1995. The new social movements revisited: Reflections on a sociological misunderstanding. In: MAHEU, L. (ed.) Social movements and social classes: The future of collective action. London: Sage.

NEPAD. 2012. Peer review mechanism. http://www.nepad.org /economicandcorporategovernance/african-peer-review-mechanism/about [Accessed September 2012]

O'toole, L. J. 2000. Research on policy implementation: Assessment and prospects. Journal of Policy Administration and Theory 10, 263–288.

Peters, B. G. and Pierre, J. 1998. Governance without government? Rethinking public administration. Journal of Public Administration Research and Theory 8, 223–243.

Rhodes, R. 1996. The new governance: Governing without government. Political Studies 44, 652–657.

Rhodes, R. 1997. Understanding governance. Buckingham: Open University Press.

Rhodes, R. W. 1988. Beyond Westminster and Whitehall. London: Unwin Hyman.

Richards, D. and Smith, M. J. 2002. Governance and public policy in the United Kingdom, Oxford: Oxford University Press.

Stoker, G. 2000. The new politics of British Local Governance. Basingstoke, England: Macmillan.

UNGA 2008. Strengthening transparency in industries (A/RES/62/274). New York: United Nations General Assembly.

UNOSAA. 2006. Natural resources and conflict in Africa: Transforming a peace liability into a peace asset [Online]. New York: United Nations Office of the Special Adviser on Africa.www.un.org/africa/osaa/reports/Natural Resources _and_Conflict_in_Africa_Cairo_Conference_ReportwAnnex es_Nov17.pdf [Accessed 3 September 2012]

Whitley, R. and Kristensen, P. H. 1997. Governance at work: The social regulation of economic relations. Oxford: Oxford University Press.

Chapter Two

Improving the Management of Mineral Resources for Sustainable Development in Africa

Kwadwo Tutu[2]

Introduction

Africa is endowed with an abundance of natural resources. It is one of the world's richest sources of minerals such as gold, diamonds, bauxite, uranium, copper and crude oil. Unfortunately, it is also the poorest continent with worsening conflicts and environmental degradation related to natural resource extraction.

In addition to their mineral and petroleum resources, most African countries also depend on the export of agricultural commodities and have done so since they attained independence, many in the early 1960s. Thus, the majority of Africa's exports are based on natural resources. Exports such as cocoa, coffee, cotton, groundnut oil, palm oil and sugar are all products that come from the land and require soil and water resources to grow. Since exports are mainly primary products, raw natural resources are the base of the economies of most African countries.

Such a lopsided trading system has consequences for the environment, revenues, economic growth and sustainable development. The dependence on commodities that are exported raw for value addition and manufacturing elsewhere has led to the decline in the Africa's share of world trade. In addition, the prices paid to African producers for many primary products have been declining in comparison with the prices of manufactured products, although there are some exceptions, including recent sharp

[2] Senior Lecturer at the Economics Department of the University of Ghana, Legon

increases in the value of some commodities, including gold and cocoa.

The reduction in its share of world trade and the deteriorating terms of trade, coupled with increasing population, are contributing factors to Africa's current status as the poorest continent. The exploitation of natural resources has also led to conflicts in many countries. In order to resolve this paradox, Africa should now look at ways to develop and ensure sustainable and equitable exploitation of its natural resources. This will address the combined problems affecting the use of the continent's natural resources, which include the limited benefit that Africa derives from them and the environmental degradation caused by extractive industries such as mining. It will also contribute to the equitable distribution of benefits of those industries for current and future generations.

This paper explores the current state of the exploitation of extractive industries, specifically mineral resources, and then looks at the role that they should play in the sustainable development of African countries. It examines ways to ensure an equitable distribution of wealth from exploitation of mineral resources between the current and future generations. In addition, it reviews the conflicts resulting from mineral exploitation and inequitable distribution of its benefits. The paper again examines the role that companies must play to ensure that their operations bring sustainable development.

Africa's non-renewable natural resources and their contribution to the sustainable development on the continent

Africa is endowed with many natural resources, both renewable and non-renewable. Renewable resources include biotic, plant and animal populations that have the capacity to grow over time, through biological reproduction. However, they can also be exhausted if they are used at a rate that exceeds their capacity to reproduce and regenerate. In addition, pollution and other adverse environmental or climatic conditions can have irreversible effects if they lead to the extinction of species of flora or fauna. Unfortunately, because of the poor management of natural

28

resources in Africa, even renewable resources such as forests, animals and water bodies are now close to being exhaustible resources.

Non-renewable resources are an abiotic and finite stock of natural resources, such as minerals, which do not have the capacity to increase in amount over time, except on geological time scale. These resources are exhaustible, so the issues of sustainability become important. Extractive industries are based on these non-renewable resources and for this reason their management and governance should ensure sustainable development of African countries.

Mineral resources in Africa

Because Africa is endowed with so many different kinds of mineral resources, the extractive sector has become the backbone of economies of many countries on the continent. Table 2.1 (below) illustrates the extent of the wealth of mineral resources in Africa. It shows that Africa ranks first in the world in terms of reserves of gold, diamond, manganese, platinum, chrome, vanadium and cobalt. In terms of production, the continent ranks first in all the listed minerals, with the exception of manganese for which it ranks second in the world. Africa is also rich in aluminium, bauxite, phosphate, oil and gas.

Table 2.1 Africa as a protagonist in mineral resources

Mineral	Africa % of World Reserve	Africa's Reserve Rank	Africa % of World Production	Africa's Production Rank
Gold	55+	1	18	1
Diamond	60+	1	54	1
Manganese	82	1	28	2
Platinum	88	1	78	1
Chrome	95	1	51	1
Vanadium	44	1	40	1
Cobalt	42	1	18	1

Source: (ECA-3, 2010)

29

In addition to those minerals in Table 2.1, Africa also provides the world with many others. About 17 per cent of the world's uranium is produced on the African continent, with almost half of that coming from Niger. The leading producer of gold in Africa is South Africa, followed by Ghana. Morocco is the leading producer of phosphate ore, accounting for 60 per cent of the continent's output. About 96 per cent of Africa's bauxite is produced in Guinea, which ranks as the world's second largest producer of the commodity. The large deposits of mineral resources in Africa represent a wealth of natural capital, which, if exploited sustainably, could turn the continent's economy around.

The contribution of mining to sustainable development in Africa

In 1987, the World Commission on Environment and Development defined sustainable development as development that meets the needs of the present generation without compromising the ability of future generation to meet their own needs. Thus the criterion for exploiting mineral resources for sustainable development requires that it benefit the current and future generations. In its analysis of the sustainable development of mineral resources, this section will examine the economic, social and environmental contributions of the sector to the economies of Africa.

Evaluation of economic pillar of sustainable development

In evaluating the economic pillar of sustainable development, the issues to be considered include its contribution to gross domestic product (GDP), Government revenues, taxes and royalties, employment, per capita incomes, exports and foreign exchange earnings and foreign direct investment.

The contribution of mining to GDP

The contribution of any economic activity to a country's GDP depends not so much on the revenues that are generated from that activity but mainly on the linkages that the activity has on the national economy. It is the backward and forward linkages that generate significant multipliers and create a larger contribution to GDP. The mining industry is capital intensive, does not generate

30

significant employment and has very few linkages due to the generally low value adding to the raw mineral resources before they are exported. As a result, there are few countries where mineral exploitation contributes a relatively high share of their GDP. In Africa, countries in the Southern African Development Community (SADC) mineral exports and their contribution to national GDPs are higher than elsewhere on the continent. On average, in SADC countries the mining industry contributes about 60 per cent of foreign exchange earnings and 10 per cent of GDP. The relatively high contribution to GDP is due to the high value addition and economic linkages in South Africa and Botswana.

Table 2.2 shows that in South Africa, because of the high amount of value addition and the linkages, the contribution of minerals to its GDP is 16.1 per cent. Without the linkages, the direct contribution of mineral resources would have been only 6.2 per cent. In Ghana, for instance, Figure 2.1 shows that the contribution of mining and quarrying has averaged just 5.3 per cent of its GDP from 1993 to 2008. For mining alone, the contribution has been a mere 4 per cent.

Table 2.2 Value addition in mining in South Africa.

Value added areas	Rand (mil)	% of GDP	No. of Jobs	% of Jobs
Direct	54 951	6.2	47 045	8.8
Indirect-backward linkage	20 315	2.3	152 947	3.2
Indirect-forward linkage	14 654	1.65	57 651	1.2
Induced	53 053	5.95	646 183	13.65
Total	142 973	16.1	1 273 82	26.9

Source: (ECA-3, 2010)

Figure 2. 1 Contribution of gold and cocoa to GDP (1993 prices) in Ghana

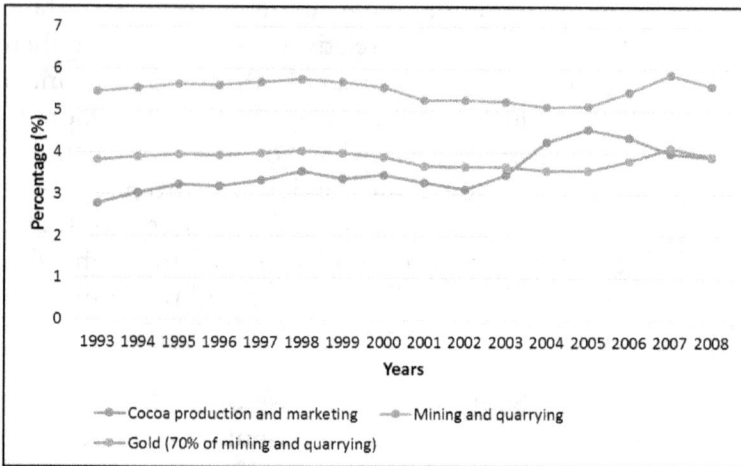

Source: (Bank of Ghana, 2010)

Contribution of mining to earnings

The extractive sector - the mining of minerals and production of oil and gas - is the economic backbone of many resource-endowed countries, accounting for a considerable proportion of foreign exchange earnings. Quantitative figures on the contribution of mining to export earnings for the various regions in Africa are presented in Table 2.3, including the Arab Maghreb Union (AMU), the Common Market for Eastern and Southern Africa (COMESA), the Economic Community of Central African States (ECCAS), the Economic Community of West African States (ECOWAS) and Southern African Development Community (SADC).

The table shows that between 1995 and 2006, the share of mineral exports of Africa's total exports has been fluctuating between 9.1 and 13.0 per cent. Of the sub-regions, mineral exports from SADC have accounted for the highest percentage of total exports.

The impressive mineral export performance of the SADC has been driven by increased mining activities in South Africa, Botswana, Zambia and Namibia, among others. As the largest gold producer on the continent, South Africa recorded at least USD 16 billion from the export of primary mineral products and USD 4.4 billion from exports of processed minerals in 2005. The economies of Angola, Botswana, the Democratic Republic of Congo (DRC), Namibia, South Africa, Tanzania, Zambia and Zimbabwe obtain between 22 and 90 per cent of their foreign exchange earnings directly from mineral exploitation. Over the decades, the performance of the other African regions has been quite disappointing; the share of mineral exports in total exports for the rest of the sub-regions showed a decline, with ECOWAS and ECCAS being the worst performers.

Table 2.3 Mineral exports contribution (%) to total exports in Africa and regions, 1995 - 2006

Year	Africa	AMU	COMESA	ECCAS	ECOWAS	SADC
1995	10.9	3.1	11.3	14.0	11.6	18.3
1996	12.1	3.3	11.5	12.5	11.3	22.6
1997	11.1	3.2	11.4	13.0	9.6	21.9
1998	10.5	4.6	16.3	14.5	9.5	17.8
1999	11.0	2.9	9.4	13.5	5.5	24.9
2000	9.1	2.1	7.1	9.8	4.9	19.8
2001	13.0	2.3	8.6	10.8	7.1	29.1
2002	10.9	2.5	10.8	10.6	7.0	23.8
2003	11.6	2.0	8.4	9.3	6.2	26.5
2004	11.5	2.1	8.8	8.5	3.6	27.3
2005	10.8	2.1	7.9	6.9	4.9	26.7
2006	12.0	2.4	9.6	5.6	5.8	29.1

Source: (ECA-3, **2010**)

It is important to note that the information presented in Table 2.3 aggregates mining contributions to total exports of African countries that are rich in resources and also those that are not. Disaggregated figures, showing results from only resource-rich countries in Africa would have shown a more significant contribution of mining to total exports. For example, in Ghana in the 1990s, the contribution of mining to export earnings averaged about 40 per cent of total exports. The corresponding figures for Angola, Botswana, Namibia, South Africa and Zambia are 43.2, 37.7, 16.3, 6.5 and 6.1 per cent respectively.

It is worth noting that mining contributes significantly to foreign exchange earnings in gross terms. However, its contributions to the economies of most mineral-rich countries, especially in Africa, are not that significant. This is because of the generous incentives given to mining firms, particularly the practise of retaining part of the sales from mineral products in foreign accounts. Specifically, lease holders are permitted by many fiscal regimes to retain a minimum of 75 per cent of mineral proceeds in offshore accounts for the acquisition of machinery, equipment, spare parts, raw materials, debt servicing, dividend payments as well as remittances of expatriate staff. This has allowed many mining companies to retain most of their earnings in offshore accounts, leaving very little in local accounts to cover local operating costs. Indeed, in many countries the little left for local purchases in real terms can be very minimal. The example from Ghana discussed below illustrates this point. In Mali and Burkina Faso, recent interviews in the finance ministries showed that the actual foreign exchange injected into those economies from mining is not more than 20 per cent of the total foreign exchange earnings (ECA-2, 2011).

Contribution of mining to government revenue

One of the main components of the mining sector reforms that were undertaken in Africa throughout the 1990s was the enhancement of the fiscal regime accorded to mining companies. By the end of 1995, about 35 African countries had revised their mining codes and made the incentive framework more attractive for mining investors. Competition among developing countries for foreign investment in the mining sector in the wake of reforms saw governments of many resource-rich African countries scaling down corporate income tax and royalty rates and offering other more specific fiscal allowances that aimed to reduce general tax liabilities of operators in the mining sector. Other sources of government income from mining, including mineral and import duties and foreign exchange taxes that contributed significantly to government revenues, were either reduced or completely scrapped. In Ghana, for instance, in its bid to attract foreign investment in its mining sector in the 1990s, the government provided generous tax incentives for foreign investors in the form of a reduction in corporate income tax, royalty rates, mineral duties and foreign exchange tax. Initial capital allowance to enable investors to recoup their capital expenditures was also increased.

These reforms created an enabling environment that allowed companies to produce at a profit. Consequently, mining industries were able to operate effectively and contribute to government revenue with corporate income tax, personal income taxes paid by mine workers as well as mineral royalties and dividends. Between 1990 and 2004, mining contributed an average of about 12.1 per cent of government revenue in Ghana. In Botswana, between 1998/99 and 2008/09 that figure was about 48.3 per cent. The relatively high contribution of mining revenue to total government revenue in Botswana is due to the high value addition to diamonds. However, apart from countries such as Namibia, Botswana and South Africa that have been adding value to their primary products, and also major oil-producing countries on the continent, in many mineral resource-rich countries in Sub-Saharan Africa the contribution from mining constitutes only 15 per cent of government revenue (Twerefou, 2009).

There is a perception that government revenue from mining in many African countries is not optimised, largely as a result of the generous fiscal incentives. Legal and fiscal frameworks intended to create a favourable investment environment have been at the expense of the capacity of states to raise revenue and they have thus constrained development (Twerefou, 2009). Another important problem for governments that depend on mining revenues is their volatile nature and the frequent downturns in commodity prices that can result in declining prices for various minerals on the world market.

Injections of foreign exchange from gold exploitation in Ghana

In Ghana, it is said that gold has been the largest foreign exchange earner since 1992, as shown in Table 2.4. However, a closer analysis shows that this is not so. The major components of total government revenues from gold exploration include corporate tax, royalties, PAYE, Construction Levy and withholding. The year 2009 saw the largest contribution of 354 million Ghana cedis or US$253 million, making 20% of total revenues (Tutu, 2010). The total foreign exchange earnings from 1990 to 2009 from gold amount to USD 19,647 million, while total revenue contribution is USD 796 million over the same period. Thus the contribution from gold to total revenue is only 4 per cent of gold's total foreign exchange earnings (Tutu, 2010).

Table 2.4 Export values and contribution (%) of key sectors of Ghana's exports

Year	Total exports (USD million)	Gold %	Cocoa production & marketing %	Timber %
1990	897	22	40	13
1991	999	30	35	12
1992	986	35	31	12
1993	1,064	41	27	14
1994	1,238	44	26	13
1995	1,431	45	27	13
1996	1,571	39	35	9
1997	1,490	39	32	12
1998	2,091	33	30	8
1999	2,005	35	28	9
2000	1,936	36	23	9
2001	1,867	33	20	9
2002	2,064	33	23	9
2003	2,297	36	36	8
2004	2,704	31	38	8
2005	2,802	34	32	8
2006	3,365	41	36	9
2007	3,216	54	35	8
2008	5,181.7	43	27	6
2009	5,882.1	43	32	3.06

Source: (Bank of Ghana, 2010)

Other payments from mining

Ghana's gold sector contributes other payments to services in the form of workers' salaries and consumables used in the mining. The sector also makes use of other inputs, including utilities. In 2009, the total value of the inputs used by the sector was USD 666.2 million, of which Ghana supplied 42 per cent or USD 278.6 million, as shown in Table 2.5. Although Ghana supplies other inputs that are not significant, this is one area where individuals and companies can make earnings.

Table 2.5 Ghana's consumption of gold consumables

Consumables	Quantity or value consumed	Total (USD)
Explosives (kilograms)	14,315,140	14,652,857.49
Fuel: diesel (litres)	94,278,601	73,478,787.27
Lubricants (tonnes)	33,632,495	5,138,060.43
Nitric acid (Analar)	30	1,954,273.10
Power, self-generated (kilowatt hours)	10,313,479	4,095,767.77
Power, national grid (kilowatt hours)	1,640,975,139	175,404,028.82
Telecommunication (USD)	39,759	1,808,309.42
Water, national grid (gallons)	22,107,677	149,431.18
Water, self-generated (gallons)	6,850,515,481	1,875,502.38
Total		278,557,017.86

Source: Minerals Commission, 2009

Foreign exchange injections into the economy in 2009

In 2009, 70 per cent of Ghana's foreign exchange earnings from cocoa was paid out to farmers. About 25 per cent was paid to government as taxes and to staff and other expenditures of the Ghana Cocoa Board. Other consumables, such as cocoa sacks and other imported inputs constituted 5 per cent of cocoa's injection into the economy. Table 2.6 shows that 95 per cent of total foreign exchange earnings from cocoa were injected into the economy, for a value of more than USD 1.7 billion (Tutu, 2010).

Table 2.6 Foreign exchange injection from cocoa and gold to Ghana's economy in 2009

Item	Foreign Exchange earnings (USD millions)	Injections (USD millions)	% of foreign exchange injected
Cocoa	1,866	1,773	95
Gold	2,984	668	22

Source:(Tutu, 2010)

For gold, total injections into the economy include consumables purchased by Ghana (USD 406 million), operating costs such as wages and salaries (USD 9 million) and others such as taxes, royalties (USD 253 million). Total injections amounted to USD 668 million in 2009. This represents only 22 per cent of total foreign exchange earnings from gold (Tutu, 2010). Thus the much-trumpeted importance of gold as the largest foreign exchange earner is in fact inaccurate, and gold's contribution to the Ghanaian economy is minimal compared with that of cocoa.

Contributions of mining to foreign direct investment (FDI)

Foreign direct investment (FDI) was cited as the major driving force behind the reforms that liberalised the mining sector in Africa. FDI has focused on the extractive sector, which in the 1990s accounted for about 65 per cent of all foreign direct investment FDI on the continent. From the 1970s when FDI inflows to Africa were a modest USD 11 billion, they rose dramatically to USD 80 billion in the 1980s and then to USD 100 billion in the 1990s (ECA-1, 2011). In Ghana, the mining's share of total FDI averaged about 67.7 per cent from 1996 to 2006 (Tutu, 2010), compared to just 22 per cent in Zambia from 2002 to 2006, as shown in Table 2.7.

Table 2.7 Share of mining in total FDI in Zambia

Year	Mining (USD million)	Total (USD million)	Share of mining (%)
2002	6,900,000	20,841,997	33.1
2003	656,766	2,941,416	22.3
2004	2,362,133	14,026,245	16.8
2007	25,000,000	293,353,300	8.5
2008	5,000,000	16,860,000	29.7

Source: Compiled with data from the Zambia Development Agency in Twerefou, 2009

In many African countries, the inflows of FDI came from large-scale mining companies employing capital-intensive extractive methods with minimal labour requirement. The proliferation of these large mining companies and procurement of large concession sites, with the crowding out of small-scale indigenous mines, have caused considerable disaffection in many mining communities.

Capital intensity of sectors

Figure 2.2 shows the proportion of FDI that goes into mining in Ghana. FDI going into the country's mining sector increased from an average of 57.5 per cent between 1994 and 2000, peaked at a high of 82.9 per cent in 2003, and averaged 67.9 per cent for the period of 1994 to 2006. For a sub-sector that contributes only 5 per cent to Ghana's GDP to receive the highest flow of FDI, while manufacturing has been dropping and receiving far less foreign investment, helps explain why the economy is not moving forward. The huge inflow of FDI into the mining sector, particularly for gold, during the 1990s was largely because of the generous fiscal regime and concessions, including tax incentives, an average foreign exchange retention rate of about 70 per cent and others.

Figure 2.2 Average share of mining in FDI in Ghana (1994 to 2006)

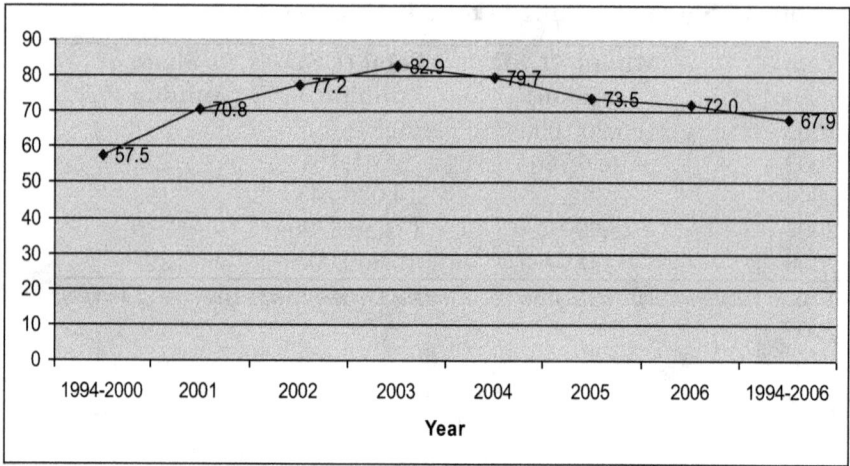

Source: (Twerefou, 2009)

Table 2.8 shows that from 1990 to 2009, USD 9,016 million was invested in Ghana's mining sector. During the same period, the total foreign exchange earned by gold was USD 19,647 million. This implies that every USD 1.00 invested in gold yielded a return of more than USD 2. During the same period, cocoa earned USD 13,919 million. With a capital intensity of USD 627 per hectares of cocoa and 1.4 million hectares of land under cocoa, the total capital invested is USD 878 million, for a return of USD 16 for every USD 1.00 (Tutu, 2010).

Table 2.8 clearly shows that gold extraction is highly capital intensive. Furthermore, capital invested in minerals in 2009 was USD 762 million while the variable cost was USD 668 million. The total cost was USD 1.43 billion in 2009. This is less than half of the USD 2.98 billion of total foreign exchange earned in that year.

Table 2.8 Flow of investment into the mining sector in Ghana

Year	Investment flow (USD million)
1990	398.24
1991	279.49
1992	595.4
1993	263.9
1994	98.33
1995	164.96
1996	774.76
1997	593.02
1998	267.54
1999	214.77
2000	231.78
2001	275.53
2002	313.72
2003	330.43
2004	556.44
2005	661.98
2006	799.5
2007	670.22
2008	765.3
2009	762.26
Total	9017.57

Source: Minerals Commission, 2009

Evaluation of the social pillars of sustainable development

The social issues of sustainable development discussed in this paper include job creation, alteration of livelihoods and health.

Contribution of mining to job creation

The contribution of mining to employment generation is variable and mostly marginal. While real incomes in the mining sector appear to be higher than the national average in many countries, the overall employment impact is limited compared with other sectors (industry, services and agriculture). This is largely because of the capital-intensive nature of mining operations.

In Ghana, industrial mining operations employed 27,481 formal workers, while small-scale mines employed an estimate of over 500,000 in 2009. This can be compared with cocoa production, which in 2009 employed about 800,000 farmers and 3.2 million farmhands, making a total estimate of 4 million people. The employment potential of the mining sector could be increased if policies were designed to encourage forward and backward linkages that have the potential to create jobs (Tutu, 2010).

Effects of mining on migration and resettlement

Unlike cocoa production, mining hand displaces a large number of communities in and around mining sites and denies them access to land, which provides both employment and livelihoods, especially for rural people. Indeed, some have argued that the net employment effect of mining is negative, if one nets out the massive displacement of small-scale miners to marginal sites as well as the abandonment of agriculture as a source of livelihoods in many rural communities.

Large-scale open pit mining by some companies sometimes requires the relocation and resettlement of communities. For example, in the Tarkwa gold mining area of southwest Ghana, a total of 14 communities involving 30,000 inhabitants were either relocated or resettled between 1990 and 1998 (Twerefou, 2009). Obviously, relocating an entire community affects its socio-economic and cultural values if mitigating measures are not taken to ensure the proper re-settlement of affected families.

One major problem with resettlement is that compensation payment for lost property is inadequate if there has not been a proper and fair evaluation of property, especially buildings, lands and agricultural activities affected by mining. Some companies prefer using the market value of houses, which may be low

42

because they are made of sand-crete or wattle with raffia leaves. However, rural communities see their property as having user values, which would mean that in the case of resettlement, they would be provided real compensation, a bedroom for a bedroom in a new home. There is also a problem providing displaced communities with alternative farmlands for farming, which is the main economic activity of all rural communities.

The rapid growth of the mining industry in Ghana has encouraged rapid migration, creating slums, health hazards, crime and promiscuity. Child labour is on the increase and it is estimated that more than 2,000 children of school-going age are engaged in small-scale mining (Mireku-Gyimah, 2011). This migration and reduction in agricultural output have resulted in high food prices and rents, causing hardship for local inhabitants. In the case of formal mining jobs, long hours of shift work in mines have resulted in family dislocation and disintegration, drug use and alcoholism among workers.

Mining and conflicts

Oil and non-oil minerals have generated significant conflicts and unrest in many African countries. The most recent significant example of this is in the Niger Delta in Nigeria. In several other countries, including Ghana, even if mineral exploitation has not generated widespread conflict, there have been localised problems where communities have tried to oppose the mining. For instance, water used in mines is drawn from rivers, lakes, underground workings or boreholes. Although this water is mostly renewable, the mine requirements in some cases exceed water availability and arouse conflicts with other users.

There are several other reasons for the conflicts caused by large-scale mining and these all relate to the fact that communities obtain minimal benefits from their operations, while they are severely affected negatively. In the first place, the exploitation begins without the communities being aware of what agreement has been concluded between governments and mining companies. These have led to serious suspicions between government officials and communities and between chiefs and their people over compensation and royalties, which in turn sometimes leads to deadly conflicts in the Western Region (Tutu, 2010).

43

In Ghana, the understanding is that the mineral deposits have been mapped out and are sold as concessions to companies without the consent of the owners of the land. Thus, people's agricultural activities are terminated without adequate consultation, discussion, negotiation and compensation. Past experience has also taught communities that they are paying the high social and environmental costs of the mineral extraction without any of the benefits or profits. A classic example of this is Obuasi in Ghana where gold has been mined for the past 100 years but there is no development in the surrounding communities to show for this. These communities do not have access to water, electricity or sanitation. There are no good public basic schools, senior secondary schools and universities. Nor are there any manufacturing firms in the mining area to provide jobs that were lost by the collapse of the agricultural sector.

Survival of small-scale mining

In many African countries, before the privatisation of mining companies, small-scale mining-although it was sometimes illegal - co-existed peacefully with the state-owned mines. For example, in Ghana the State Gold Mining Corporation in Tarkwa had a special arrangement with small-scale miners, under which portions of the company's concessions were given to them for mining. In return, the small-scale operators sold their products to the mines at a special price.

The restructuring of the mining sector in the mid-1980s that resulted in de-emphasis of government's interest in mining and in cost-cutting measures adopted by the privatised mining companies, have meant large-scale retrenchment. Since those people laid off have no source of livelihood other than mining, many of them have resorted to small-scale mining on concessions of the large mines, causing significant environmental destruction and pollution. There has not been any attempt on the part of many governments to organise and train these small-scale miners. Their survival is at risk as they are attracting negative attention and reports about their activities.

Impacts of mining on health

In the area of health, the flow of liquid and gaseous pollutants to the environment around the mines can pose health and safety risks for those inhabiting the environment as well as nearby settlements. Among others, these pollutants include emissions such as sulphur dioxide from processing plants, run-offs from mine processes and leakages from rock and tailing dumps that contain various elements and chemicals that are quite detrimental to human health. Inhaling large amounts of siliceous dust and poor quality air in the mines is one of the major health hazards among miners. Gold-mining activities usually produce silica-rich dust particles that can cause silicosis and tuberculosis as well as aggravate respiratory diseases such as asthma. In areas where surface mining and small-scale mining, vector-borne diseases such as malaria and schistosomiasis are common. This is largely due to the stagnant ponds that provide breading grounds for mosquitoes and blood flukes.

Gold mining, especially by small-scale miners, poses serious health risks to the miners and the communities in which they operate. It is estimated that gold 'panners' use about six tonnes of mercury annually. About half of the mercury is lost through the amalgamation process and careless handling, making it a major health risk to mining communities. The health risk posed by mercury increases when 'panners' dilute the mercury with water to increase quantities; mixed with water, mercury is very detrimental to human beings and plants.

Evaluation of environmental pillars of sustainable development

Although mining has the potential to provide a variety of socioeconomic benefits, its environmental and social costs, if not well handled, can lead to massive deforestation, land degradation, habitat alteration and water and air pollution. It is generally accepted that in Africa the mining sector is second only to agriculture as a source of pollution. The mining sector is resource-intensive, generating high concentrations of waste and effluents. Kuhndt et al. (2008), for example, argue that from the extraction process through to smelting, the production of one tonne of copper generates 100-350 tonnes of residues, 50-250 tonnes of extraction waste, 200-900 of mineral dressing waste and slag, up to 300 kilograms of sulphur dioxide and uses 30-100 Gigajoules of energy.

From the exploration stage through to the closing of a mining operation, mineral extraction impacts seriously on the environment. These impacts can be direct, through the value chain of activities: prospecting, exploration, site development, ore extraction, mineral dressing, refining/metallurgy, smelting, transportation, and post-mining activities. There can also be indirect impacts through the environmental degradation caused by adjustments in and sociocultural development of communities in mining areas. Environmental problems arising from mining include air pollution, discharge of silt and waste into surface and ground water, land and forest degradation, noise pollution, solid and liquid waste disposal, as well as the generation, storage, transportation and disposal of toxic substances. There are also environmental health issues that have been addressed in the previous section on the social pillars of sustainable development. All these activities have negative effects on sustainable development, as well as on livelihoods and thus require urgent attention. In the following sections we elaborate on the environmental impacts of mineral extraction.

Air pollution caused by mining

Various activities in the mineral value chain produce gases that pollute the environment. Many mines transport the ore to the processing site and use a lot of fossil fuel in the production process. The combustion of fossil fuels generates sulphuric, carbonic and nitric acids, as well as other volatile organic compounds and heavy metals that pollute the environment. These gaseous compounds combine with water in the atmosphere and come back to the earth in the form of acid rain. Acid rain has the potential to destroy natural and built-up areas, particularly structures made from marble and limestone, such as monuments.

Fossil fuels also contain radioactive materials, mainly uranium and thorium, which are released into the atmosphere. In 2000, it was estimated that about 12,000 tonnes of thorium and 5,000 tonnes of uranium were released worldwide from the burning of coal, and some of these emissions came from extraction activities (ECA-3, 2010). Coal gasification and combustion in underground mining pollute the atmosphere, while aluminium smelting and refining processes produce effluents such as sulphur dioxide, slugs and chemicals and generate hydrogen fluoride (HF) in the molten electrolyte process. (ECA-3, 2010).

Water pollution caused by mining

Mining impacts on water through all the phases of mining activity, including during the actual extraction process, seepage of contaminated water from mine residue deposits resulting from mineral processing/beneficiation, de-watering during active mining operations, and re-watering (flooding) of closed mine voids, and the discharge of untreated mine water.

Many gold-mining companies practise the heap leach method of gold beneficiation. This has the potential to contaminate ground water, while the use of mercury by small-scale miners contaminates surface water. Also, in underground mines, water pollution results from in-situ leaching caused by leakage into aquifers and discharge of wastewater. Additionally, run-off of sodium cyanide from leach pads may contaminate local streams used by mining communities, while leakage of cyanide-gold-bearing solution through the heaps pollutes ground water. In order to reduce cyanide leakage and pollution, High Density Polythene (HDPE) is used. However, it has been shown that the HDPE has a high rate of seepage caused by pinhole leaks and poor seaming techniques (ECA-3, 2010).

Pollution of local rivers and streams is significant in mining areas, caused by discharge of mine waste, accidental bursting of tailings dams, dredging and sluicing, and this includes both large-scale and small-scale mines. In Tarkwa in the Wassa West District of Ghana, the accidental burst of a tailing dam in 2001 led to the release of thousands of cubic metres of mine waste into the Asuman River, contaminating the river with cyanide and heavy metals. Since this river is the main source of drinking water for the communities in the area, about a thousand people were denied access to good drinking water. Much aquatic life, including fish and crabs, were killed. Rivers such as the Ankobra, Offin and Densu in Ghana have been seriously polluted by mining activities, making them unsuitable for domestic use (Twerefou, 2009).

47

Studies of mining sites elsewhere in Africa show similar negative environmental effects. A study undertaken near a Fluorspar Mining Plant in Kerio River Valley revealed that iron levels in the river were about three times those recommended by the World Health Organisation. The levels of fluoride and heavy metals emitted into the environment from the Fluorspar Mining Plant in Kerio Valley were also high. In Zambia's Copper belt, effluent from the mines ends up in the Kafue River, a source of drinking water for about 40 per cent of the country's population (ECA-3, 2010).

Another significant environmental problem in mining communities is acid mine drainage, or the outflow of acidic water from mine sites. This can be caused by the oxidation of waste rock that contains sulphide or rock used in road construction in mining areas. Acid mine drainage has a high propensity to degrade soils, pollute aquatic habitats and allow heavy metals to seep into the environment. Many countries, including Ghana, South Africa, Zambia and Zimbabwe, have either reported the occurrence of acid mine drainage or the susceptibility of their mine environments to acid mine drainage (ECA-3, 2010). Boocock (2002) reports that in the United States in 1998 the cost of remediation of acid mine drainage, which affected some 20,000 kilometres of watercourses, was estimated to be between USD 2 and 35 billion.

Aquifer dewatering for mines, characterised by the excavation of vast lands and the creation of large craters, reduces the ability of boreholes, streams and hand-dug wells to recharge, leaving most of them unproductive or with reduced yields. This phenomenon has been felt in the mining area around Tarkwa in southwest Ghana. In the Copper belt of Zambia, the competing demands of the mining industry and of the communities in the mining area for resources-especially water, energy and food - have led to the unsustainable use of water resources (ECA-3, 2010).

Chemical pollution caused by mining

Large-scale mining generally produces large volumes of waste and chemical pollutants that may affect vast tracts of land and have devastating impacts on ecosystems. Hazardous chemicals used in the mining sector include heavy metals and mercury, among others. When not properly managed during production, transportation, application, storage and disposal, these heavy metals and chemicals can contaminate soils and water, important habitats for aquatic life, and then enter the human food chain, with deadly consequences (UNEP, 2006).

Mercury, which is mainly used in gold extraction, especially in small-scale gold mining is a poisonous substance and its toxic effects include damage to the brain, kidney and lungs. Mercury has a long life, remaining in these organs for about 30 years after their ingestion. In 2005, about 3,439 tonnes of mercury were used globally and 29 per cent of this was attributed to gold extraction by small-scale mining. A map of mercury emissions in Africa shows that they are concentrated in the continent's mineral belts, stretching north from South Africa through Central to West Africa, and then to North Africa. The highest concentrations of mercury emissions appear in countries with extensive extractive industries, in South Africa, Zimbabwe, the Democratic Republic of Congo, Nigeria, Ghana and Algeria (ECA-3, 2010).

Onshore and offshore petroleum exploration and exploitation also cause serious pollution of coastal environments. A study on the quality of seafood resources and sediments of the Qua Iboe River estuary and mangrove swamps in Nigeria revealed serious pollution due to offshore petroleum activities such as solid waste dumps and frequent oil spills on the biotic resources and overall ecological disturbances (ECA-3, 2010). Analysis of petroleum hydrocarbons and heavy metal loads revealed that mean metal levels in benthic sediments were higher during the wet than dry seasons, although both were above average concentrations. In general, the levels of heavy metals and total petroleum hydrocarbons (TPH) in the estuary were high compared with similar ecosystems in the rest of the world.

Land degradation caused by mining

Evidently, a vast majority of the rural poor in Africa derive their livelihood directly from the rich natural resources on the surface, farming the land, harvesting abundant food, medicine and other resources from forests, from hunting and fishing, and other related activities. Both small- and large-scale mining degrades lands and forests, which are the major sources of livelihoods for local communities. Mining destroys the vegetation, including economic timber species and the natural forest regeneration of all age classes. It also degrades the land, rendering it unproductive through the removal of topsoil and other activities. Mining activities cover vast areas through the prospecting and exploration phases, including pits and trenches, mine site surface facilities, mine surface excavations, amenity buildings, processing plants, storage sheds, dumps and dams, as well as residential and commercial areas, water and sewage treatment plants, and access roads and railways. These activities all require removal of vegetation and the deforestation results in soil erosion and overall land degradation.

Processes involved in mineral dressing lead to the creation of effluent and tailings dumps and ponds, which also occupy large tracts of land surface. The tailing dumps and ponds usually contain heavy metals and other chemicals such as cyanide and thiosalts (Sulphur oxides) that have a high potential to degrade land. Many African countries do not collect data on tailing dumps created by mining, making it difficult to know the actual area on the continent that is covered by tailings. A report by the South African Department of Environmental Affairs and Tourism (2005) indicates that in 1997, mines generated about 471 million tonnes of mine waste, slime dams and waste rock dumps covering about 47,000 hectares. The report further notes that over 200,000 hectares of natural habitat have been transformed by mining activities. The situation is quite similar to that in the Copper belt of Zambia. Over time, the mining industry in Zambia has accumulated about 32 overburden dumps containing about 1,899 million tonnes of overburden, covering an area of about 206,465 hectares. Also, there are about 21 waste rock dumps containing about 77 million tonnes of rocks and covering an area of about 388 hectares. Furthermore, there are about 45 dumps/dams containing about 791 million tonnes of tailings, and covering an area of approximately 9,125 hectares (Sikaundi, 2008).

Many mining companies construct railways and roads to mining sites and sometimes through isolated areas. The construction and use of these railways and roads can have adverse effects on wildlife, depending also on traffic density and types of users. When they are built though isolated and protected areas, they can have major impacts on game animals such as lechwe, impala or warthog, in that it opens up their habitat and exposes these animals to hunters, while also making hitherto remote rivers more accessible to commercial and sport fishermen. In some cases mining in or near aquifer rocks has caused water problems and earthquakes (ECA-3, 2010).

Africa covers an area of close to 30 million square kilometres, more than 3 trillion hectares, of which about 21.8 per cent is forested. This accounts for about 16.8 per cent of the global forest cover. With a net loss of about 4 million hectares annually, Africa is the continent with the second largest net loss in forest cover. Nigeria and Sudan were the two largest countries with the highest loss in natural forest during the period 2000 to 2005, largely as a result of subsistence agriculture (ECA-2, 2011)

Almost all activities in mining lead to the destruction and degradation of forest resources. Land clearance for construction in mine sites leads to forest degradation and soil erosion, causing sediment loading in water bodies and the non-protection of watersheds. Deforestation also causes a reduction in carbon sequestration, which is needed to combat global warming and climate change. The destruction of large areas of forest as a result of surface mining and the use of wood as support structures in some mines have caused substantial reduction in communities' access to fuel wood and charcoal, on which many rural populations depend on for their energy requirements.

Environmental cost of mining

While proponents of mining point to the economic benefits that the extractive sector can have for a country, less attention is generally paid to the significant social and environment costs of mining. These costs are not always adequately captured for the simple reason that valuations of some environmental costs have not been calculated. Probably, the best approach to assessing environmental impacts would be to assign monetary values and market prices to what is lost, damaged or destroyed in the environment. Unfortunately, such an approach, while useful in theory, is very difficult in practice because of distortions in prices and market imperfections. In developing economies and especially in Africa, market prices are even more distorted with the extremely uneven distribution of wealth and access to resources. Also, the irreversible losses due to over-use or misuse of resources are difficult to value in monetary terms. The problems with valuation are aggravated by the lack or limited knowledge of the interrelationships between the various biological elements and with the ecosystem, and how economies interact with the environmental system.

Mireku-Gyimah (2011) attempted to estimate the cost of mitigating environmental degradation caused by mining. His estimates show that this could be as high as 30–100 per cent, or even more, of the total cost of a mining operation, depending on the geological and environmental settings of the mineral deposit. In contrast, the cost of managing Corporate Social Responsibility (CSR) ranges from just 10 to 40 per cent of the total cost of mining, depending on the vital needs of the community. This is an important effort to assess the real environmental costs of mining, but there is still need for much more research in this area.

Optimal management of mining industries

There is some ambiguity as to what mining companies ought to do to optimise their value to local communities and host countries, apart from just paying corporate taxes. In this vein, there has been considerable debate about the issue of CSR. Under CSR, some companies provide services such as infrastructure and other activities to benefit mining communities. Some companies have provided roads, railways, water, power, medical and education facilities in mining areas. In Ghana, for instance, AngloGold-Ashanti has made investments in sporting facilities, including a sports stadium, while Goldfield Ghana Limited sponsored the Ghana national team in the 2006 Football World Cup in Germany and the 2010 World Cup in South Africa. In South Africa, the mining industry invested in the 2010 World Cup in South Africa through additional infrastructure to drive and sustain economic growth. In Zambia's Copper belt, many infrastructural developments have been undertaken by mining companies for the use of mining communities (Twerefou, 2009).

While these CSR activities are important, it must be emphasised that they should not distract from, compromise or diminish the sole objective of ensuring that governments obtain a significant proportion of mining earnings so that they can undertake sustainable development activities. Governments have key roles to play in ensuring sustainable development. Thus, they must make every effort to secure adequate returns from mining activities in their countries and use these revenues appropriately for development. This means that long-term sustainable development strategies should be formulated that can take care of both the long-term benefits and costs of mining activities. It is only in this way that governments and policy-makers can ensure that the long-term benefits significantly outweigh the costs of mining.

Such strategies should take into account all the issues along the entire value chain of mining processes and activities, and plan for the type of human skills that will be needed in the long term for the mining industry chain. This will also include the building of local entrepreneurial capacity to exploit these mineral resources in the long run. The strategies should also take care of research, technology and innovation for the extractive industries. The issues of what kind of capital needs to be mobilised to prevent financial liability on future generations should also be considered. In the case of Ghana's oil and gas, the plan to ensure the use of modern household energy systems, with a greater percentage of households connected to and provisioned with gas, demands that long-term strategies should be urgently considered. Finally, there is the imperative of undertaking natural resources accounting as part of a green economy to ensure that natural resources are efficiently and sustainably utilised. Significant research on the costs and benefits of mining should be undertaken to enable governments to negotiate with companies to ensure that African governments and the people they represent receive adequate returns of the profits of companies and do not bear of all costs (social and environmental).

Environmental governance

We have noted above that the urgency to attract investments to Africa gave significant benefits to mining companies under the structural adjustment programmes of the 1980s. While these effectively encouraged investment in mining, they placed less emphasis on addressing environmental degradation caused by mining activities. However, since the 1990s, many governments have established environmental agencies and have enacted Environmental Impact Assessment (EIA) policies and laws. New and existing mining projects are now required by law to provide an

EIA and Environmental Management Plan (EMP). To some extent, EIAs have helped countries to do better evaluations of the benefits and costs associated with mining and to adopt measures, such as restoration and rehabilitation, to avoid and mitigate harmful impacts. For example, with the help of an EIA, South Africa was able to stop the development of a titanium mine along the eastern shores of St. Lucia, an area renowned as a valuable source of biological diversity. The area was declared a World Heritage Site in 1999 (ECA-3, 2010).

Many governments have made it a policy to continuously review the institutional, legal, fiscal and financial regimes under which mining operates to ensure international competitiveness and relevance to national development goals, including equitable sharing among all parties of the benefits derived from mining. Zambia, for example, reviewed the windfall tax to increase government revenue in the 2008 budget (Twerefou, 2009). Although much has been done in the areas of legislation to better address the environmental and social problems arising from mining, implementation of these laws has been very weak. There are various reasons for this, including a lack of coordination among mining support sector institutions, inadequate capacity of environmental protection authorities, and the weak EIA and monitoring process.

Weak coordination among mining sector institutions

Mining has adverse environmental effects on local resources, including land, air, water and forest. Cumulatively, these then have negative impacts on livelihoods and on the social structure of mining communities. Therefore, there is a need for a multi-stakeholder approach when it comes to governing mining operations and investment policies. Unfortunately, coordination among the sector institutions is quite weak. In many countries, the effective involvement of forestry, land and environmental ministries, departments and agencies in the granting of mining licences is quite weak. More importantly, chiefs, opinion leaders and the community as a whole are not adequately involved in investment negotiations in the mining sector.

Weak implementation of EIAs

EIAs for mining operations are mandatory in several mineral-rich African countries. However, their effective implementation is hindered by inadequate scoping, baseline studies and low community participation, which are essential to the process. Although many EIAs make scoping claims, the socioeconomic, cultural and environmental problems that were meant to be addressed through scoping still persist in many mining projects for which EIAs were prepared.

Discussions with environmental officials suggest that there are major loopholes in the EIA process. In some cases, consultations are held with key individuals, particularly chiefs and opinion leaders, who are mostly beneficiaries of royalties and benefits but are not directly or adversely affected by the project. It is also alleged by mining communities that such consultations are used as public forums where the benefits of mining activities are extolled, while the potential negative effects are played down. Furthermore, where the community has raised concerns during such consultations, it is common to find such concerns deliberately overlooked by the mining firms.

Additionally, even when the EIA reports are made available for public comment, their technicality makes it difficult for the rural communities, where populations are mainly illiterate and semi-illiterate, to understand. There are also provisions in some environmental guidelines that exempt companies from obligations to accept all recommendations of an audit report, and the fact that many environmental agencies treat environmental monitoring or audit reports as confidential, and these have to some extent rendered the process a mere formality. As a result, some mining communities have come to see EIAs as a mere conditionality that they only need to respect when they are trying to acquire financing for their activities from International Financial Institutions (IFIs), and not a binding document and mechanism to ensure that mining is conducted in a sustainable manner.

Weak capacity of the environmental protection institutions

Institutions responsible for the development, implementation and oversight of environmental protection regulations are constrained by inadequate human, technical and financial capacity to fulfil their mandates. This is unfortunate given the operational definition of the environment, which is quite broad in scope and coverage and therefore requires adequate resources and capacity to safeguard a healthy environment. In Ghana for example, the mining department of the Environmental Protection Council has eight experts overlooking all mining activities in the country. The department is ill-resourced to undertake the monitoring and evaluation of environmental degradation and to subject EIAs and other environmental reports to critical verifications

Conclusion and recommendations

The substantial mineral endowment of African countries could make an enormous contribution to sustainable growth, development and poverty reduction, provided sector linkages are made with other sectors of the economy, as well as ensuring that EIAs are mandatory and effectively enforced. Experience in countries such as Botswana, Namibia and South Africa suggest that the effective participation of all stakeholders in extractive industries' investment and the mineral cycle can reduce risks of future conflicts and assist in optimising the contribution of mining to sustainable development and poverty reduction. Additionally, through enhanced mineral rents, mining could contribute significantly to the development of all sectors of the economy.

An overall recommendation for ensuring environmental sustainability and sustainable development in the exploitation of minerals is the creation of a process and environment in which stakeholders in the mineral value chain undertake activities that enhance the durability and productivity of minerals and metals, while minimising risks and costs. The implication of this stewardship is that mining companies should undertake responsible product design, use, reuse, recycling and disposal of their waste.

It must be noted that while it is possible to achieve a balance between mineral exploitation and the reduction of social and environmental impacts of mining, this is not an easy task. However, it is an essential policy direction if we are to ensure sustainable exploitation of African mineral resources. The multidimensional nature of the problem suggests that measures should be multi-faceted, inculcating legal, institutional and administrative changes by all stakeholders as well as co-operation from all stakeholders. At the regional level, such measures should include but not be limited to:

- Enhancing support for continental, Regional Economic Communities and country initiatives to revise and reform mineral regimes. This will help create equitable and sustainable mineral wealth from an integrated and diversified mining industry that optimises linkages.

- Improving regional cooperation with development partners to facilitate systematic geo-mapping in order to define known assets and delineate new ones.

- Establishing capacity for the identification and facilitation of the forward and backward direct linkages of mining with other sectors of the economy, particularly, investment in mining inputs, beneficiation and physical infrastructure.

- Establishing resource-based development corridors through public-private partnerships (PPPs) that optimise the indirect linkages through the collaborative use of the mineral infrastructure such as transport, power and water to enhance other sectors - agriculture, forestry and resource processing sectors of the economy.

- Providing support at the national and regional levels for the identification, management and prevention of conflicts related to mining operations

- Developing a continental energy strategy for harnessing Africa's vast hydro-electric power potential (e.g. Congo River Basin) through a continental transmission grid, to cater for the increasing demands from the mining sector and to replace fossil fuels in other sectors. For countries, a hybrid of energy including solar, wind, thermal and nuclear could be considered.

- Harmonising mining regimes among countries and economic communities in Africa, especially fiscal regimes, to avoid a 'race to the bottom' competition.

- Locating resources for the effective functioning of continental partnerships/initiatives. Establishing a continental fund for world-class transaction Advisers for the negotiation of large mineral contracts with long tenure.

- Establishing mineral venture capital facilities to enable African entrepreneurs to invest in the mineral sector.
- Ensuring the effective implementation of the Kimberley Process Certification Scheme (KPCS) in member countries and the establishment of similar regulatory systems for other minerals to address the issue of 'conflict minerals'.
- Facilitating the adoption and application of minerals' conventions emanating from KPCS, the EITI, EITI++, as well as other systems such as the International Council on Mining and Metals (ICMM) toolkits and codes for hazardous substances (mercury and cyanide).

At the national level, policies must include but not be limited to:

- Developing fiscal regimes that enhance revenues and their efficient use for the communities and the nation to address inter-generational equity.
- Developing effective institutions that reduce rent seeking, corruption and ensure effective participation of all stakeholders, monitoring, transparency and accountability.
- Developing appropriate artisanal small-scale mining regimes that facilitate sustainable mining.
- Identifying and setting up effective conflict prevention and resolution mechanisms, including arbitration.
- Establishing mineral development funds (from mineral revenues) to ensure sustainability through investment in human resources, research and development to enhance value addition at all stages of the mineral value chain.

References

Bank of Ghana. 2010. Ghana exports data. Accra: Bank of Ghana.

Boocock C. N. 2002. Environmental impact of foreign direct investment in the mining sector in Sub-Saharan Africa. Paris: OECD

ECA-1. 2011. Review report on progress towards sustainable development in Africa. Addis Ababa: United Nations Economic Commission for Africa.

ECA-2.2011. Review report on progress towards sustainable development in West Africa. Addis Ababa: United Nations Economic Commission for Africa.

ECA-3.2010. Trade, mineral exploitation and sustainable development in Africa. Addis Ababa: United Nations Economic Commission for Africa.

Kuhndt, M., Tessema, F. and Martin, H. 2008. Global value chain governance for resource efficiency building sustainable consumption and production bridges across the global sustainability divides. Environmental Research, Engineering and Management 3, 33–41.

Minerals Commission, 2009. Production of minerals in Ghana, Accra: Minerals Commission

Mireku-Gyimah, D. 2011. To mine or not to mine: The economic controversy and its resolution. Ghana Academy of Arts and Sciences Inaugural Lecture. Accra.

Sikaundi G. 2008. "Copper mining industry in Zambia. Environmental challenges". unstats.un.org/unsd/ environment/envpdf/UNSD UNEP. /Session%2008 5%20Mining%20in %20Zambia%20(Zambia).pdf

Tutu, K. A. 2010. Trade for sustainable development: The story of cocoa, gold and timber in Ghana. Accra: Institute of Economic Affairs (IEA).

Twerefou, D. 2009. Mineral exploitation, environmental and sustainable development in EAC, SADC and ECOWAS Regions. Addis Ababa, Ethiopia: ECA

UNEP. 2006. African environmental outlook 2: our environment, our health. Nairobi, Kenya: United Nations Environment Programme.

Chapter Three

Social Policy and State Rev enues in Mineral-Rich Countries in Africa

Madonna Afiba Dolphyne[3]

Introduction

Social policy is an integral part of economic growth. Many studies claim that mineral resources impact negatively on economic growth, particularly in developing countries. This chapter briefly reviews this argument (the natural 'resource curse' hypothesis) and analyses its implications for development in mineral-rich countries in Africa. The discussion considers mineral endowments, an implicit form of capital with the potential to spur socio-economic growth if critical challenges for the equitable distribution and management of the mineral wealth are handled appropriately and the revenues are invested in infrastructure, facilities and services that improve living standards, particularly those in communities in the mining areas.

It articulates the conditions, success factors and strategies that can maximise the contribution of the mineral sector to growth and development in Africa. These are needed to: create a conducive and competitive policy, legal and regulatory framework for business development; to improved governance and management systems anchored on strong and capable institutions; to open up opportunities and sharpen investment decisions promoting linkages between the mineral sector and other sectors of the economy; to empower communities, and: to establish coalitions of change and facilitate knowledge and competencies for efficient management of mineral wealth. This chapter also aims to raise awareness among policy-makers and practitioners about the

---

[3] Executive Coordinator, Centralian Consulting Foundation, Ghana

development issues and public policy challenges of managing mineral wealth to promote growth and reduce poverty in Africa by offering some policy options and strategies for addressing these challenges.

Investments in the extractive industries can contribute to sustainable development if the benefits from mining are well used. Notable initiatives to improve governance in the extractive industries include the 'Publish What You Pay' (PWYP) campaign and the Extractive Industries Transparency Initiative (EITI). Several guidelines, protocols, codes of practice, organisational policies and management systems, voluntary undertakings and statements of principle have been instituted to help improve sustainable development in the minerals sector. There is a better understanding now of what it means and what it is required to promote sustainability in mining. This bodes well for the future of mining.

Mr Horst Köhler, former President of Germany and head of the International Monetary Fund, in delivering the inaugural address at the official launch of the John A. Kufuor Foundation at the University of Ghana in September 2011, observed that Africa had an enormous quantity of natural resources that could provide a great source of economic prosperity for the continent. But, he cautioned, 'the crucial task will be to ensure that this fortune will benefit all people' and thus be a blessing instead of a curse. He stressed the need for the continent to develop a strategy that would make the best use of its natural resources, what he described as a 'sustainable resource-based African growth and development strategy'. Such a strategy requires respect for the rule of law, good governance, effective anti-corruption policies and a host of other best practices.

The natural resource 'curse' argument

Mining has been under scrutiny for quite some time, with many feeling that the costs of mining outweigh its benefits, particularly in developing countries. Some constituencies have, for example asked the World Bank Group to stop financing the sector. There are two distinct schools of thought. On one hand are those that view mineral resources as an endowment that has the potential to spur growth and development in developing countries. On the other side are those who argue that mineral resources are a 'curse' and that, in general, growth in mineral-rich and dependent economies have been worse than in countries endowed with fewer minerals. Those who adhere to the latter point of view are not persuaded about the role of mining as a growth engine and posit that much of the mining in developing countries is a capital-intensive enclave industry, foreign-owned, operated largely by expatriates, and that it relies on inputs (especially equipment) that is purchased abroad. In addition, they state that output, income and employment multipliers in mining, as well as its learning-by-doing potential, are lower than in other sectors, such as manufacturing. Chapter 2 of this book provides an elaborate discussion on this argument.

Accordingly, the boom and bust nature of mining is said to engender poor development performance and sub-standard welfare and social indicators. The proponents of the 'resource curse' hypothesis further observe that the record of oil- and mineral-rich states in alleviating poverty is worse than that in states with similar levels of income, but little or no oil and mineral wealth. These scholars suggest that the pattern of underperformance in mineral economies could be linked to growth inhibition caused by several factors that work in tandem. Among these are the 'Dutch Disease' (Cordon and Neary, 1982), endowment-related alliances with powerful vested interests in securing control of mineral rents, the decline and instability in the terms of trade for mineral commodities, a lack of local capacity to predict the magnitude of government revenues and foreign exchange earnings and hence to plan expenditure and investment, allowance for profligate social and infrastructure spending, which usually continues even when reserves or revenues decline, and the enclave nature of mining (Auty and Mikesell, 1999, Philips, 2002). Some have suggested that political underdevelopment may be at the root cause of the underperformance of mineral economies (Karl, 1997 and Heller, 2006). Others contend that resource booms produce a false sense of security, overconfidence and illusions of plenty among policymakers and tend to weaken state institutions (Nwete 2004). In that vein, Philips (2002) notes, 'when mineral development occurs in a context of underdeveloped social, political, and economic institutions, the non-renewable resource

63

wealth tends to be squandered, the level of social conflict increases and nearly irreparable damage is inflicted on the environment'. He further emphasises that these developments can leave a developing nation permanently poor.

The argument is that in sub-Saharan Africa, abundance of mineral resources can accelerate the route to poverty and many reasons are given for this: human capital creation and accumulation is neglected; governments are not responsive to the needs of the poor; social infrastructure is weak; economic policy is dysfunctional; rent-seeking prevails; corruption reigns; public income is squandered by the elite in power and those close to it, and; wars of attrition and conflicts are common (Auty and Mikesell, 1999, Philips, 2002, Nwete, 2004a, Nwete, 2006). Common characteristics of African countries affected by 'Dutch Disease' are low inclusive growth, corruption and high socioeconomic inequality. Most of these countries are highly exposed to economic shocks due to their lack of diversification and the cyclical nature of commodity prices. These complicate the implementation of pro-poor and growth enhancing policies and make it difficult to reduce poverty. The fact is, poor people in mineral-rich countries are more vulnerable and exposed to risks and that of itself should speak for pro-poor extractive resources development and management in mineral-rich African countries.

Success stories of some mineral-rich countries

However, the picture is not all bleak in Africa. There are some success stories to learn from. Referring to the role mineral resources play in the development of Canada and Australia, Philips (2002) argues that mineral-led industrialisation in those countries was not driven by the mineral sector per se, but by an 'overall transformation in business and financial organisation, education, research and knowledge development, human capital accumulation and infrastructure expansion'. He affirms that well-developed and stable political institutions that respected the rule of law, markets and private enterprise played an equally important role in fostering this industrialisation.

Where mining has contributed to better development outcomes in Africa, as is the case in Botswana, Morocco, Namibia and South

Africa, success has been linked to a host of factors, including: sound management of the sector; good governance; respect for the rule of the law; good infrastructure, and; an overall favourable environment for business development. Botswana is an excellent model of a resource-rich economy in Africa using revenues related to natural resources (predominantly from diamonds in this case) to escape the 'resource curse' through prudent macroeconomic management. Botswana developed its own system for reinvestment of mineral revenues to offset depletion, the Sustainable Budget Index that requires that all mineral revenues be reinvested. In the process Botswana has achieved remarkable improvements in infrastructure, human capital, and the basic services supplied to its population (Philips, 2002, ECA, 2004)

Some policy options for mineral-rich countries in Africa

It is therefore important to understand these attributes of mineral resources, the daunting public policy challenges that they pose, as well as the limitations that they impose on policy makers and other stakeholders. These challenges are linked to:

- Creating a viable, integrated and diversified mining industry throughout the value chain, and sustaining mineral wealth without compromising environmental, social and cultural considerations, and ensuring a regulatory framework that encourages mineral creation (the creation challenge).
- Investing transitory mineral revenues to ensure lasting wealth and deciding how much ought to be saved and how much should be invested and in what (the investment challenge).
- Distributing benefits from mining equitably, balancing and managing conflicting local and national-level concerns and interests and deciding what form the allocation should take to promote pro-poor growth (the distributional challenge).
- Ensuring sound systems of governance and a stable macroeconomic policy, which curbs rent-seeking and corruption, addresses issues such as 'Dutch Disease' and externalities such as unstable commodity prices, and

enhances public interest in wealth conservation (the governance and macro-economic challenges).

This chapter contends that where economics, social and environmental considerations are properly addressed, mineral resources should not be left in the ground. Instead, they should be exploited judiciously, using the highest corporate, social and environmental standards to ensure better development outcomes. Because mineral resources are finite, mineral wealth should be invested to create new wealth and used to create forms of renewable capital, human, social and physical, which are key to achieving sustainable development beyond the mining. It is also important to develop mineral clusters and to create opportunities for growth of lateral or downstream businesses that have the potential to create more employment and generate valued-added rents and wealth. In countries where mining is an important, if not the dominant sector of the economy, or where it has the potential to be so, strategies to address the creation, investment, distributional, governance and macroeconomic challenges of mineral resources management should thus centre on:

> Creating a conducive, stable and predictable policy, legal and regulatory framework and a competitive fiscal regime with a view to attracting and retaining the required level of investment in the sector, creating wealth, promoting employment and opening-up opportunities.

- Achieving better allocation of revenues from mineral resources and redistribution of the benefits of mineral wealth through improvements in the governance and management of revenue flows derived from mining, and through decentralisation of decision-making and resource allocation.

- Promoting a calculated, parsimonious and well-informed spending, savings and investment (in other assets) strategy, which prioritises human, social and physical capital creation and transformation of mineral wealth into financial assets that yield higher returns (the annuity policy).

- Promoting the stabilisation of mineral resources revenue and reducing fiscal imbalances through greater fiscal discipline, a certain level of fiscal conservatism and increased capacity for forecasting and managing mineral revenues with a view to reducing uncertainties about their magnitude, mitigating market externalities and minimising adverse macro-economic impacts associated with commodity price fluctuations.

- Enhancing governance systems, organisational and institutional capacity, particularly in the ministries of finance and planning, and in local governments.

- Forging tri-sector partnerships and creating coalitions of change among public, private (mainly mining companies) and local stakeholders to improve community livelihoods and to maximise other socioeconomic and development outcomes.

- Empowering communities in mining regions so they are able to make informed decisions and better participate in their own development.

- Unbundling the sector and promoting a strategy that encourages local procurement and outsourcing of goods and services, value-addition and local beneficiation of minerals, diversification from minerals, and that also optimises business multipliers and enhances linkages between mining and other sectors of the economy, including at the local community level.

- Encouraging mining companies to behave in a more social and corporate responsible manner with a view to improving the social relevance of mining. The strategies described above are general in nature. To render them relevant, their application should be context and country specific, taking into consideration local capacity and resources (financial, technical and above all human skills and knowledge), as well as constraints. To be effective, the policies should be part of an overall poverty reduction and growth strategy and should be mainstreamed in comprehensive and sound Poverty Reduction Strategy Papers (PRSPs) or other development plans. To better capture and factor in the PRSPs the mining dimension and variables, there is a need to adequately profile the mining sector and to develop a thorough understanding of the positive and negative impacts of mining for poverty

67

reduction and growth promotion.(Philips, 2002, Pegg, 2003, ECA, 2004, Päivi, 2005, Nwete, 2006).

Improving local participation in mineral resources development

Given the current societal-oriented development paradigm, this chapter advocates that the development of mining should be people-centred and not only profit-motivated. In this quest, new partnerships, conscious of the need for change, are emerging and being built between governments, the corporate world, civil society, local communities and other stakeholders. The multilateral partnerships could be advanced through collaborative governance, as this book advocates. Guidelines, protocols, codes of practice, organisational policies and management systems, voluntary undertakings and statements of principle are being drafted and enforced to help effect this transition and improve the social and development outcomes of mining at the local level. However, more needs to be done to achieve change. Policies, legal and regulatory frameworks to facilitate equitable participation by local business people, communities and other stakeholders in mining activities should be in place, as should tools to improve at the local level the distribution of revenue derived from fiscal instruments such as royalties, income taxes, land taxes, and lease rents. The key areas that should be addressed include: preferential employment of local labour; contracting of services and procurement of goods from indigenous local companies; provision of infrastructure to local communities; allocation of benefits from mining to local communities; local community allocation of national revenue; and community equity participation. If local communities are to participate in and benefit from any form of collaborative governance arrangements, these issues should be integrated into the policy-making and implementation processes.

In developing a framework for facilitating public participation at the country level, there is need therefore to consider and factor in the local context and peculiarities. Because each country is different and specific, the approaches described below should serve only as references.

- The Papua New Guinea Act of 1992, which stipulates that a minimum of 20 per cent of royalties received by the government should be paid to landowning communities of the mining lease area (In this case royalties are paid directly by mining companies to the agreed beneficiaries and then reconciled to central government for auditing).(World Bank, 2006).

- Special Support Grants (also in Papua New Guinea) paid to a given provincial government, which represent about 1 per cent of the gross value of mineral sales of companies operating in that province.

- Preferred Area Status (also in Papua New Guinea), which requires companies to provide preferential treatment in terms of employment, education and training and business development assistance to communities in the area in which the company mines. (World Bank, 2006, Orogun, 2009).

  The holding of mineral rights to platinum and other resources by local peoples, as is the case with the Bafokeng people of the small Royal Bafokeng Nation in northwest South Africa. The Bafokeng Nation is a shareholder in the Impala Platinum Holdings Ltd, which is the second largest producer of platinum in the western world. The company has four mines, namely Bafokeng North and South and Wildebeestfontein North and South (World Bank, 2006)

- Local Impact and Benefits Agreements (IBAs) involving mining companies, government and communities where mining development occurs on traditional lands or in remote communities. The IBAs can range from ensuring employment and training of members of the local community to equity participation and profit sharing.

- The scorecard for a broad-based, socioeconomic empowerment charter, such as the South Africa Mineral and Petroleum Resources Development Act (Act No. 28 of 2002), which sets targets for South African mining companies to transform the face of the mining industry in the country in terms of human resources development, employment equity, migrant labour, mine community and rural development, housing and living conditions, procurement, ownership and joint ventures, beneficiation, and reporting (World Bank and International Finance Corporation, 2002, Van Vuuren, 2006).

To empower local communities to effectively and meaningfully participate in the development of mineral resources in their constituencies, there is the need to enhance their capacity through training and improvement of their rights of access to information. Participation should also be extended to policy formulation, as well as planning and monitoring of project implementation. Environmental impact and social assessments should be mandatory for all project approval processes.

Mainstreaming mining in PRSPs

As indicated in the World Bank framework and reiterated by Philips (2002) and Nwete (2006), when integrating mining into a PRSP or Interim -PRSPs, policy-makers should focus on gathering relevant data to understand actual and potential poverty-related impacts, as well as risks and opportunities of the mining sector in their country. They should also setting clear objectives and identify priorities for intervention in a consultative process regarding poverty impacts and the mining sector. Additionally, they should identify the mechanisms to achieve the objectives, including needed changes in policies, laws and regulations. And finally, they should establish the necessary institutional arrangements, including authorities, responsibilities and capabilities, to implement the mechanisms.

In preparing the PRSPs there is need to foster broad consultation and participation by involving representatives from local communities and local governments from mining regions, industry associations, trade unions, non-governmental organisations (NGOs), and other relevant parties. In most cases, the ministry responsible for mining is well placed to lead the process. In addition, the inputs and participation of medium-and large-scale mining companies should be sought, as they have resources and expertise that can play a vital role in creating sustainable development opportunities.

Fostering minerals cluster development

It is appropriate to reiterate the importance of a strategy to promote minerals cluster development (ECA, 2002, ECA, 2004). Such a strategy looks at broadening the economic base and developing linkages between mining and other sectors upstream, downstream and side-stream on the value chain ladder, and at maximising development and social outcomes. It includes all industries and services that gravitate to mining, such as financial services, transport, communication, energy, water, engineering and design, other consultancy services, knowledge and research and development centres, providers of capital goods and consumables. Some of the key outcomes are as follows.

- increasing local upstream support (supplier/input industries) sectors
- enhancing downstream industries based on increased local beneficiation and value addition of goods
- facilitating lateral migration of mining technologies to other industries
- increasing social, human, knowledge and institutional capital (which can be used in other sectors)

For this concept to be realised and effective, it is important to have a shared strategic vision, deliberate, purposeful and proactive collective action (with governments taking the lead), timely interventions, and also coordination of public, private and community interests at all levels. There is a need to identify, at national and regional levels, areas where such clusters could be developed and to devise strategies to facilitate project implementation. It is important not to underestimate the role of regional cooperation and integration in reducing transaction costs, establishing intra-regional synergies, enhancing competitiveness and realising economies of scale that would catalyse mineral cluster development. However, for goods, services, capital and other factors to freely flow in the regional spaces, there is a need to expedite intra-regional harmonisation of laws, regulations and fiscal regimes. Some other critical factors that can spearhead minerals cluster formation are as follows.

- availability and further development of a local skills base

71

- adequate infrastructure
- existence of a critical mass of companies and institutions willing to cooperate, network and share knowledge and information formally (e.g. through industry associations such as Chambers of Mines) and informally
- combination of legal requirements and incentives that encourage local outsourcing of goods and services
- provision of financial support for the development of small-and medium-scale mining supply and services companies
- existence of hives of research and development, innovation, diversification and technology diffusion;
- establishment of programmes for targeted human resources development and technical support systems
- establishment of effective marketing channels, which can improve demand

Artisanal small-scale mining (ASM) provides a good framework for the development of the mining sub-sector in Africa. The vision of mineral cluster development recognises ASM as a poverty-driven activity and recommends that it should be integrated into PRSPs of African governments. It further urges that the mining policies and laws of member states in Africa should be reviewed to incorporate a poverty reduction dimension in ASM strategies (ECA, 2002, ECA, 2004). Equally important is the framework provided by the 2004 – 2006 Strategic Plan of the Communities and Artisanal and Small-Scale Mining (CASM), the global forum for knowledge sharing and coordination between the various institutions working on ASM. CASM's vision on ASM is one that:

- Advances integrated rural and regional social and economic development;
- Functions within an equitable and effective legal framework;
- Establishes positive, productive relationships with local communities, as well as with large-scale mining companies and government agencies;
- Utilises environmentally-responsible techniques;
- Complies with international standards related to child labour and occupational health and safety;

72

- Provides an acceptable income through increasingly productive mining and processing practices;
- Allows for long-term efficient resource extraction;
- Accesses fair markets and sources of credit, and;
- Enhances local infrastructure and services.

There is therefore a need to mitigate the environmental, social and economic factors that create poverty in ASM communities and to integrate ASM into local and regional economic development and land-use planning, to promote cooperation for constructive change and build synergies between ASM and large-scale mining, and lastly, to provide training to small-scale miners in analytical skills, sound business and management culture, capabilities and practices. This will help to scale up ASM and to facilitate its transformation from a transitory and shock-or-coping-response activity into a serious business venture. It will also help to change ASM communities from vulnerable and marginal enclaves of unorganised groups of miners and other actors, into integrated and functionally sustainable and resilient communities. (ECA, 2002, Nwete, 2004a, Nwete, 2006)

Conclusion

In conclusion, there is scope for other African countries to learn from and emulate successful examples like the one offered by mining success in Botswana, where the mineral sector, in this case diamonds, has played a pivotal role in the growth and development of the country. Good governance is a fundamental prerequisite for transforming mineral endowments in other mineral-rich African countries into a blessing that can promote growth and poverty reduction. There is a need to shift from resource extraction to resources management. Because mining does not happen in isolation, the overall context of any country's economic management and the strength of it institutions are both important in ensuring sustainable mining. Therefore, for mining to play a constructive role in African economies, at the country level there is a need for an overall transformation in business and financial organisation, education, research and knowledge development, human capital accumulation and infrastructure expansion. This is at the core of the minerals cluster concept advocated in this chapter.

This can be achieved in an environment of well-developed and stable political institutions that respect the rule of law, markets and private enterprise. In the African context, to achieve this will be a daunting task. Other key requirements to mainstreaming mining into growth and poverty reduction are good mineral policies, laws and regulations and a balanced fiscal regime that promotes the creation of mineral wealth. In addition, to promoting equity and fair distribution of the benefits of mining, there is also the need to enhance transparency, accountability, oversight and monitoring in the management of mineral revenue flows and decentralisation of revenue sharing. Furthermore, extractive industries need to be unbundled to increase local beneficiation and value addition. In addition, local procurement and outsourcing of goods and services would help diversify and create more employment and value added rents and wealth. Governments have to play a proactive role in this effort.

Sustainability of mining can be enhanced if mineral wealth is invested in the creation of human and social capital and partly in an income-generating portfolio of financial assets that yield higher returns than mining. Additionally, development outcomes of mining can be enhanced if coalitions of change are promoted. These would involve increased, informed and meaningful participation of local communities and other stakeholders in the decision-making and implementation of extractive industry projects. This should be coupled with better understanding and factoring of local context and specificities, and better integration of mining in local economies, development plans and poverty reduction strategies (e.g. PRSPs). For this to be done effectively, it is necessary to strengthen institutional capacities and competencies (at government and other levels) for efficient long-term planning that promotes sustainable development, prudent management and smart spending, savings and investments of mineral wealth.

References

Auty, R. M. and Mikesell, R. F. 1999. Sustainable development of mineral economies, Oxford: Clarendon University Press.

Cordon, W. and Neary, J. 1982. Booming sector and de-industrialisation in a small open economy. The Economic Journal 92, 825–848.

ECA.2002. Compendium on best practices in small-scale mining in Africa. Addis Ababa: United Nations Economic Commission for Africa.

ECA.2004. Minerals cluster policy study in Africa: Pilot studies of South Africa and Mozambique. Addis Ababa: United Nations Economic Commission for Africa.

Heller, T. C. 2006. African transitions and the resource curse: An alternative perspective. Economic Affairs 26, 24–33.

Karl, P. I. 1997. The paradox of plenty: Oil booms and petro-states. Los Angeles: University of California Press.

Nwete, B. 2004a. How can tax allowances promote investment in Nigeria's petroleum industry? Oil, Gas and Energy Law Intelligence 2, 1–15.

Nwete, B. 2004b. Transnational corporations and the project: Any hope for human rights and sustainable development? Oil, Gas and Energy Law Intelligence, 2, 1–15.

Nwete, B. 2006. Legal and policy framework for promoting petroleum expertise in Africa. African Petroleum Producers Association, International Seminar. Algiers.

Orogun, W. 2009. Audit queries 'missing' N162bn in oil sector. NBF News, 10 August 2009.

Päivi, L. 2005. A diamond curse? Civil war and a lootable resource. Journal of Conflict Resolution 49(4): 538–562.

Pegg, S. 2003. Poverty reduction or poverty exacerbation? .World Bank Group support for extractive industries in Africa. Report sponsored by Oxfam America, Friends of the Earth-US, Environmental Defence, Catholic Relief Services, Bank Information Centre, Washington, DC.

Philips, D. 2002. Petroleum revenue management: An overview. Washington DC: World Bank. ESMAP Programme.

Van Vuuren, H. 2006. Time to listen to Lesotho! The World Bank and its new anti-corruption agenda. Bretton Woods Project.

World Bank. 2006. Papua New Guinea. http://www.worldbank. org/data/countryclass/classgroups.htm#Low_income [Accessed 07/06/01 2002 SRC - GoogleScholar].

World Bank and International Finance Corporation. 2002. Large mines and local communities: Forging partnerships, building sustainability. Washington, DC.

Chapter Four

Analysis of Governance in the Ghanaian Mining Sector

Abdulai Darimani[4]

Introduction

In most African countries, the legal regime defines mineral resources as public goods. In Ghana, Chapter 21, Article 257, Clause 6 of the 1992 Constitution, as well as Clause 1 of the Minerals and Mining Act, 2006 (Act 703), make mineral resources the property of the Republic 'vested in the President in trust for the people of Ghana'. The public ownership of mineral resources provides rights, responsibilities and obligations for citizens and communities. It also brings together multiple actors whose interests may not only stand in opposition to each other's, but also undermine the larger public interest. An investment in a mining project may take place in a site adjacent to a community or cluster of communities. Such an investment necessarily brings together the mining company (large or small), the state and the community, all of whom seek to maximise their own particular interest: the state for foreign exchange earnings, revenue and protection of public interest including the environment; the investor for profit; and the community for their livelihoods, well-being and social protection.

The fact that extractive resources are public goods for which there is competing interest from multiple actors makes governance central in any discussion about their sustainable extraction and processing, as well as their equitable distribution and effective utilisation. Again, the 'public good' nature of extractive resources

---

[4] Environment Programme Officer, Third World Network-Africa Secretariat, Ghana

means they are subject to contestation. In the area of mining, not only are there conflicts over control, distribution and utilisation of the mineral wealth but also about the impact of mining on specific interest groups. For instance, as companies try to maximise profit, they externalise environmental cost to communities and host governments. History is replete with incidents of violent conflicts and civil wars in Africa that are fought over the control of mineral resources. The Democratic Republic of Congo, Sierra Leone and Liberia are examples of countries affected by violent conflicts caused or fuelled by struggle for control of mineral resources. Over the years, concerns have been expressed about the disproportionate distribution of the mineral wealth between mining companies, host governments and local populations affected by the mining project. Concerns have also been expressed about the legacy of negative environmental and social consequences of mining. Aryee et al. (2011), point out that the negative environmental consequences of mining, especially of the older mines, have been substantial. Protecting the environment and ensuring a balance of the multiple but opposing interests, while permitting a mining project to go ahead, is the heart of governance.

Mining in Ghana

Ghana is an important mineral-producing and -exporting country. Minerals such as gold, manganese, diamonds, bauxite, limestone, silica salt and salt are being exploited in commercial quantities in the country (Akabzaa, 2009). Gold, however, is by far the largest commercial mineral in Ghana. In Africa, Ghana ranks second, after South Africa, in the production of gold. Table 4.1 shows the annual mineral production of Ghana for four commercial minerals for the period 1990 – 2009. In addition to these minerals, in 2007 oil was discovered in commercial quantities in Ghana and the country has since joined the committee of oil-producing nations in Africa.

Table 4.1 Annual mineral production of Ghana (1990 – 2009)

Year	Gold (ounces)	Diamonds (carats)	Bauxite (megatonnes)	Manganese (megatonnes)
1990	541,147	636,503	368,659	246,869
1991	847,559	687,736	324,313	311,824
1992	1,004,625	656,421	399,155	276,019
1993	1,261,890	590,842	364,641	295,296
1994	1,438,483	746,797	451,802	238,544
1995	1,715,867	631,708	530,389	187,548
1996	1,583,830	714,738	383,370	266,765
1997	1,752,452	829,524	536,723	332,703
1998	2,371,108	822,563	341,120	384,463
1999	2,608,102	681,576	355,263	638,937
2000	2,457,152	878,011	503,825	895,749
2001	2,381,345	1,090,072	678,449	1,076,666
2002	2,236,833	963,493	683,654	1,135,828
2003	2,274,627	904,089	494,716	1,509,432
2004	2,031,971	905,344	498,060	1,597,085
2005	2,138,944	1,065,923	606,700	1,719,589
2006	2,337,784	972,992	972,991	1,699,546
2007	2,628,290	836,488	1,033,368	1,305,809
2008	2,796,955	599,007	574,389	1,261,000
2009	3,119,832	354,443	420,477	1,007,010

Source: MSSP, 2011

In the early 1980s, the government of Ghana undertook massive reforms of the mining sector, which were unprecedented in the history of the country. The reforms have resulted in a significant increase in mining activities. From the inception of the reforms in 1983 to date, the sector has witnessed a considerable investment boom and an increase in the number of new mines and mineral properties at the development and advance exploration stages, particularly in the gold sub-sector (Akabzaa, 2009). As of January 2009, 225 local and foreign companies held concessions for reconnaissance, prospecting, and mining leases in Ghana (Minerals Commission of Ghana, 2009). These concessions stretch offshore into Ghana's territorial waters from Cape Coast through Takoradi to Axim, and then weave through a greater part of the entire western corridor from the coast through to Hamile at the Burkina Faso border in the Upper West Region. In addition, the sector has attracted a large number of mining support companies that provide goods and services, such as catering, transport, security, explosives, mineral assay laboratories and drilling. The expansion in the activities of mining has resulted in increased production of various minerals in Ghana, and expansion that is illustrated in Table 4.1.

Conceptualising governance

Collaborative governance has emerged as a form of governance for addressing the environmental and social challenges, as well as the economic inequality inherent in mining. According to Cleaver and Franks (2005), governance is characterised simultaneously by a diversity of definitions. Hamdok (2003) describes governance as a '"framework" for interaction in which the actors involved exercise their rights, meet their obligations and articulate their interest'. This definition draws attention to the importance of the involvement of actors in ways that guarantee their rights and interests. Dwivedi (2002) looks at governance as a system of values, policies, and institutions by which a society manages its economic; political, and social affairs through interaction within and among the state, civil society and private sector. The definition makes the point that governance does not happen in a vacuum but is linked inextricably to issues and values, and that it takes place within or outside the locus of the state.

In terms of scope and character, governance may have two broad dimensions - technical and political (Graham et al., 2003, Campbell, 2004, Darimani, 2011). The technical dimension addresses questions of effectiveness and efficiency of systems and institutions in the delivery of goals and objectives. The political dimension, on the other hand, focuses on building and improving relations between and among actors. Governance may also be characterised as good or bad. On the one hand, doing things right, such as adhering to the principles of participation, accountability, fairness, transparency, equity and justice, may lead to a characterisation of the governance process and content as good. On the other hand, non-adherence to these principles may also lead to a characterisation of governance as bad. Even where such principles are adhered to, governance may still be characterised by specific actors or groups as good or bad, depending on the nature of the results or outcomes of the governance process and content on specific actors and groups.

Whether good or bad, governance involves rules of conduct, leadership, activity and process (Hyden and Court, 2002), which operate in various contexts and modes. Collaborative governance is one of the modes of governance that brings multiple actors together to engage on issues and processes that advance their individual and collective interests. The multiple actors may include state or non-state actors, or both. Ansell and Gash (2007) define collaborative governance as 'a type of governance in which public and private actors work collectively in distinctive ways, using particular processes, to establish laws and rules for the provision of public goods'. This chapter adopts and modifies this definition of collaborative governance, which it sees as a form of governance in which state and non-state actors work collectively and in distinctive ways, using particular rules and processes to protect their individual and collective interests, as well as to manage and distribute the risks and benefits of economic activity.

Collaborative governance is increasingly becoming popular in the field of development generally, and particularly in the mining sector. In the last few decades, there has been an increase in the amount of development discourse involving governments and development practitioners involving citizens, communities and civil society. Indeed, much of the past decade has seen democratic expansion and consolidation, particularly in Africa. This democratic framework is expected to provide the conditions for participatory processes, including the forging of partnership arrangements. At the international level, one of the major outcomes of the World Summit on Sustainable Development (WSSD) held in 2002 in Johannesburg, South Africa, was Type II informal collaborative arrangements and partnerships. Although not a new concept, the Type II outcomes formally asserted the importance of collaboration and partnerships as key mechanisms for achieving the goals of environmental governance and sustainable development (Darimani, 2011).

Demand for collaborative governance is on the increase. Zadek (2005) argues that 'Everyone wants to collaborate; even those who do not want to work together want to be seen to be willing, at least in principle if not in practice. The media landscape is saturated with calls and demands for partnerships, alliances, coalitions and networks. There is a growing number of multi-actor initiatives such as coalitions of NGOs in the extractive sector. Among them are the African Initiative on Mining, Environment and Society (AIMES), the Tax Justice Network, Publish What You Pay (PWYP), and Ghana's National Coalition on Mining (NCOM); the Extractive Industries Transparency Initiatives (EITI); the Extractive Industry Review (EIR); Community Development Funds (CDFs) and the Global Reporting Initiatives (GPI). These coalitions and groups are gaining crucial grounds for better management of the benefits and risks of mining projects. They work alongside the collaborative approaches dictated by the legal regime. For instance, the administration of the framework of environmental impact assessment (EIA) has become the heartbeat through which African governments secure governance in the mining sector.

Statement of the problem

The growth in collaborative governance in the mining sector is meant to redistribute power, minimise inequality in the distribution of the mineral wealth, enhance environmental protection and curb the incidence of conflicts and human rights violations caused by mining. It is through such governance that societies vest current generations with hope that they can effectively address the challenges of poverty, inequality and environmental insecurity (Zadek, 2006).

This does not appear to be the case in the mining sector of Africa. Despite the vast mineral resources and growth in governance, there is widespread poverty and income inequality in mineral-producing and -exporting countries on the continent. Indeed, poverty and income inequality are sometimes much worse in communities adjacent to mining projects in Africa. Concerns have been expressed about the marginal economic benefits of mining to such communities. These range from the disproportionate benefits earned by foreign mining companies compared with the host countries and local communities, the inadequate transparency and accountability in the relations between companies and national governments over the transfer and use of mining revenues, and the lack of value-addition and linkages between mining enclaves and the rest of the national economy. The fiscal regime for mining in most mineral-endowed African counties have been shown to provide huge incentives to foreign investors in mining, which simply legalise capital flight out of the national economies of mineral-producing and exporting countries. The decision by the African Union (AU) to reform the mining regimes on the continent was prompted by the disproportionately large benefits for foreign mining companies compared with those for national governments (ECA, 2007).

In addition, there are concerns about the negative impacts on livelihoods and the environmental and social disruptions caused by mining. Mining projects result in involuntary resettlement, relocation, displacement, and seizure of private property without adequate compensation. The negative environmental, economic and social impacts of mineral extraction often result in the violation of the human rights of people in communities affected by the mining (Commission on Human Rights and Administrative Justice, 2008). The human rights violations include assault, harassment, shooting, inhuman treatment and deprivation of livelihoods.

Research questions and purpose

The key questions posed by this chapter are:

- Do all actors benefit from governance in mining?

- Does governance enhance equitable distribution of the mineral wealth in Africa?

- Is governance good for environmental management in the mining sector?

- What actions are required to enhance governance in Africa's mining sector?

This chapter explores and assesses these questions with a focus on the role of public policy strategies in Africa's extractive sector. Public policy determines the terms and conditions under which mining takes place, regulates the practices of actors and confers powers on regulatory institutions. It also has the potential to control environmental destruction, redistribute wealth and influence the practices of actors involved in mining. Because of this, a reasonable a priori assumption is that impediments to governance for enhanced management and equitable distribution of the wealth of extractive industries and environmental management in Africa is very much a result of the nature and implementation of public policy. This is to suggest that there is a limit to the extent to which governance can achieve equitable redistribution of the benefits and risks of extractive sector activities. In short, public policy is central in any search for effective solutions to the challenges of extractive industries in Africa.

Research design and methodology

This chapter has been designed around a qualitative study. The research relied principally on a review of literature on environment, mining and governance in Africa's extractive sector. Brief overviews, based on secondary data, were made of the general pattern of state policies on mining. The research and this chapter also draws on results from a previous study of the effectiveness of environmental governance in mining communities of Obuasi and Birim North Districts of Ghana to analyse the research questions and study objectives. Finally, the paper benefitted from participant observation at relevant meetings and conferences as well as inquiries, consultation and responses to issues and debates about extractive industries and governance in and for Africa. The research was conducted from August to October 2011.

Results and analysis

From the research, evidence emerged of different forms and categories of governance in the mining sector and these are summarised into five categories in Table 4.2.

The different forms and categories of governance appear to be in response to a number of conditions. Darimani (2011) outlines the essential conditions, which include: (1) the pervasive nature of environmental problems associated with mining; (2) the need to enhance the countervailing power of politically weak actors, such as local communities and women's associations; (3) the ascent of the doctrine of participatory environmental management; (4) the

84

benefit of pooling limited resources for optimum results; (5) weaknesses of the regulatory framework or its failure; (6) public pressure, and: (7) the desire by for-profit mining companies to appear to be good corporate citizens.

The different forms and categories of governance are initiated by different actors in the mining sector. For instance, citizens' groups and NGOs form coalitions and networks as particular forms of collaboration in response to the challenges that mining poses to communities and nations. Examples of these networks are AIMES, initiated by Third World Network-Africa in 1999 as a Pan-African mining sector advocacy network; Ghana's NCOM launched in 2001 as a national network that brings together communities and NGOs to engage in mining sector advocacy in Ghana. There are also other CSO and NGO networks such as PWYP, Revenue Watch, and the Tax Justice Network-Africa.

Private mining companies promote governance initiatives at the local, national and international levels. At the local project level and through the processes of environmental impact assessment, mining companies set up various committees aimed at addressing community concerns of their operations.

Table 4.2 Categories of governance initiatives found in mining

Category	Description	Actors involved	Target Issues	Example
Public-public	collaborative arrangement between and among state institutions	State Regulatory Agencies Missions of governments Inter-governmental institutions	Political effectiveness Cost efficiency	EPA and Minerals Commission exchange data on mine safety Foreign Missions facilitate entry of home company
Private-public	Formal and informal arrangements between state actors and non-state actors	State Private investors Communities Civil society Inter-government institutions	Mineral wealth Environment Community concerns/livelihoods Public interest	Administration of Environmental & Social Impact Assessment (ESIA) brings many actors together; EITI Natural Resource Annual summit
Private (for profit and non-profit)	Collaborative arrangement between non-state actors involving non-profit civil society organisations (CSOs) and profit organisations	Private profit seeking companies Charity organisations	Transfer of skills and knowledge (in most cases from the charity organisations in support of the profit motives of private companies)	Mining companies contract NGOs to provide various services, including training of communities

				Alliances/Coalitions/Networks of CSOs and NGOs
Private (non-profit)	Collaborative arrangement between and among non-profit civil society organisations and voluntary associations	CSOs NGOs Community-based Organisations (CBOs) Voluntary groups	Capacity Countervailing power Strengthened roles	
Private for profit	arrangement between two or more profit-making organisations	Profit-making companies	Cost efficiency Technology transfer Profit maximising	Global Reporting Initiative

Source: Field work, 2011

Some of the committees that are common in the mining sector of Ghana include Compensation Negotiation committees, Crop Rate Review committees and Resettlement and Relocation committees. These committees bring together a variety of social groups and individuals to determine the appropriate approaches and issues for ameliorating the social, livelihood and environmental impacts of mining.

At the national and international levels, mining companies come together to develop initiatives aimed at addressing the impact of their operations. The Global Reporting Initiative is an example of a governance initiative by private mining companies. There are also other governance initiatives involving citizens groups, governments and private companies at the national and international levels. The EITI is an illustration of a governance initiative involving citizens' groups, mining companies and governments. In Ghana, the natural resource summit, launched in 2009, has become a platform for collaboration among governmental agencies and their development partners in Ghana, CSOs and private mining companies. While not specific to mining alone, the ESIA has been an important instrument for governance, involving as it does citizens' groups, mining companies and governmental agencies.

It was observed that governance arrangements in the mining sector of Africa have produced some important outputs, including: the transfer of experiences, skills and inputs; consensus-building, and; providing communities with appropriate channels to articulate and pursue their interests and concerns. For instance, civil society networks and coalitions have been an important platform for expressing concerns about mining and for demanding accountability of government and mining companies. People from communities affected by mining that participate in coalitions and civil society networks and NGOs are well able to articulate their concerns about mineral resource allocation in public meetings. The natural resource summit, which was launched under the natural resources and environment governance programme in Ghana, has become a platform for exchange of experiences and a joint review of the programme's implementation. As noted earlier, the GRI is an outcome of long years of collaboration between mining companies and industry practitioners.

Despite their existence and their respective outputs, governance initiatives have not yet made any notable changes to the fundamentals of mining regimes operating on the continent. Serious poverty and income inequality in mineral-producing and - exporting African countries and in communities in mining areas are widespread on the continent. The World Bank actively led the reforms of the mining sector in Africa, with the argument that the current liberalised mining regimes were to catalyse growth and development by increasing foreign investment and exchange earnings, government revenue, employment creation and transfer of skills and technology, among others. Yet, over two decades of implementing the liberalised mining regimes, the World Bank (2006) has admitted that the number of people living in extreme poverty in Africa almost doubled, going from 164 million in 1981 to 314 million in 2000. In 2000, the World Bank (2006) calculated aggregate genuine saving rates by regions, which revealed that the genuine saving rates recorded by sub-Saharan Africa regions consistently hovered around zero. The Bank argues that as resource rents (mainly minerals and oil) increase as a percentage of Gross National Income (GNI), genuine saving rates tend to decline, implying that a significant proportion of natural resource rents are being consumed, rather than invested in other productive assets, FDI in the mining sector of Africa has been on the increase. It was up by 5 per cent in the mid-1980s, and by 15 per cent in 2004. According to the United Nations Conference on Trade and Development (UNCTAD), this placed Africa third in the investment league, behind Latin America and Oceania (United Nations Conference on Trade and Development (UNCTAD), 2005). It is not only the World Bank that recognised the marginal contribution of mining in Africa. At a roundtable conference held in February 2007 in Addis Ababa, Ethiopia, representatives of African governments and policy officials concluded that the continent had not benefited from the liberalised mining regimes. The correlation between the mining boom and increased poverty highlights the inequality of earnings between mining companies and host governments.

Ghana, a trailblazer of the liberalised mining regimes, epitomises the income inequality in the distribution of mineral wealth. This inequality appears at several different levels: between mining companies and central governments; between central governments and local government and communities, and; and within communities. As noted in the previous paragraphs, transnational mining companies are the main beneficiaries of the mineral wealth of Africa, including Ghana. The Minerals Commission of Ghana (2004) reports that mining accounts for an average of just 11.8 per cent of government revenues and large-scale mining accounts for just 2 per cent of formal direct employment. The sector's contribution to the country's GDP is just 5 per cent (Minerals Commission, 2004). Many have argued that these figures posted by the Minerals Commission show that mining contributions are marginal and do not correlate with the expansion in the production of various minerals (Akabzaa, 2000, UNCTAD, 2005). According to UNCTAD (2005), when figures provided by the government on the total value of mineral exports are compared with income (revenue) derived from mineral taxes, it shows that Ghana earned only about 5 per cent of the total value of exports, i.e. about USD 46.7 million out of a total mineral export value of USD 893.6 million, based on 2003 calculations.

The relatively minor contribution of mining to Ghana's economy is a direct result of state policies for mining. Since the project to reform and liberalise Ghana's mining sector in the early 1980s, the primary emphasis of state policy for the mining sector has been to attract more and more transnational capital. The government is pursuing this objective by providing a stable legal and fiscal framework, which includes a mining code, contractual stability, a guaranteed fiscal regime, profit repatriation, and access to foreign exchange (Campbell, 2004). For instance, custom duties and value-added tax (VAT) are exempted on mining equipment. All class-three assets of mining companies, such as plants and machinery, buildings at the mine project camp, and exploration/prospecting expenditures, benefit from an 80 per cent capital allowance for the first year of mineral production and 50 per cent in subsequent years. The exploration/prospecting expenditures are capitalised (converted as capital expenditure) and deducted from the income of mining companies before tax. Mining companies are also permitted by the fiscal regime to carry forward losses for a period of five years, and they enjoy deed of warranty, which means that certain expenses made in foreign accounts that they are permitted to operate do not attract income tax.

Dividend payments to government for its automatic equity participation have been marginal, erratic and fading. In 2005, dividend payments accounted for 17 per cent of total mining receipts; it fell to 12 per cent in 2006, then to 6 per cent in 2007 and a year later they were down to just 1 per cent (Ministry of Finance, 2010). This is because dividend payments are solely a management policy under the laws of Ghana. Therefore, some mining companies take advantage of this policy and do not declare dividends accruing to government from its equity participation. As part of the stabilisation for private mining companies, the Ghanaian government has entered into stability agreements with two of Ghana's major gold mining companies (Newmont Ghana Gold Limited-NGGL and AngloGold-Ashanti-AGA). These agreements limit the amount of royalties payable to government to just 3 per cent for a period of 15 years. According to the Bulk Tax Unit of Internal Revenue Service interviewed in October 2011, the Ghanaian government continues to charge a royalty tax of only 3 per cent on the two companies, even as the gold price is currently high and the royalty tax has been raised to 5 per cent.

In effect, the nature of state policy for mining has led to increased inequality, which in turn deepens poverty. The booming minerals sector has simply crowded out jobs for thousands of rural farmers that have been dispossessed of their land. Meanwhile, only a small number of workers (2 per cent of all formal jobs in Ghana) are benefiting from direct formal employment in large-scale mines in the country. Furthermore, most of these workers are employed on short-term contracts with limited labour rights. The inability of the state to raise sufficient revenue makes government a perpetually aid-dependent economy, which also has implications for policy autonomy and the capacity to regulate.

Despite modest benefits to and improvements in employment, incomes and standards of living of mining communities, the booming mineral sector has generated numerous negative environmental impacts of great concern. Exploration, development and production of the mines, as well as the processing of minerals, result in pollution of water by chemicals and waste, atmospheric pollution by noise and dust, degradation of land through excavations and waste piles, and destruction of the vegetation. In addition, mine facilities such as airstrips, buildings,

91

roads, tailing and cyanide spent dams, as well as migration to the area and increased human activities exert considerable pressure on the biophysical environment, leading to loss of biological diversity. Several streams and rivers in mining areas in Ghana are either polluted or rendered unhealthy because of mining activities. Considerable amounts of farmland are also lost to mining and the rent paid for such land is ridiculously low, at 0.50 Ghanaian Cedis [USD 0.23] per square kilometre (km^2) of land. The low value for land translates into multiple losses for landowners, who are deprived of their title, the use of the land and its vegetation and their intrinsic value.

The main sources of revenue from mining are: (1) dividends accruing from state equity participation; (2) income taxes such as pay as you earn or P.A.Y.E), property rates, ground rents, profit taxes and excise and import duties, and; (3) royalties. Royalties are unique, the biggest and most predictable source of revenue from mining. Of the total benefits received from mining, royalty payments alone constituted about 84 per cent in 2004; 57 per cent in 2005; 53 per cent in 2006; 68 per cent in 2007; and 64 per cent in 2008 (MSSP, 2011). In addition to the other taxes, the central government takes the biggest share (80 per cent) of royalty payments from private mining companies (Table 4.3).

Table 4.3 Distribution of mineral royalties

Beneficiary	Percentage (%) share of total royalties collected
Central government consolidated Fund	80
Minerals Development Fund	10
Local government and communities	10
Total	100

Source: Field Work, 2011

The 10% that is allocated for local government and communities is further divided among the District Assembly (local level representative of government), Office of the Administrator of Stool Lands, the stool and the traditional council in the proportions outlined in Table 4.4.

92

Table 4. 4 Distribution of the 10% at the level of local government and communities

Beneficiary	Share of the 10%	Share of the 10% converted to 100%	Remarks
Office of the Administrator of Stool Lands	1	10	For administrative cost
District Assembly	4.95	49.5	The mine must be in District
Stool	2.25	22.5	The mine is in traditional stool/council area
Traditional Council	1.80	18	
Total	10	100	

Source: Field Work, 2011

Our research also found a disproportionate distribution of the environmental burdens of mining. While local communities in mining areas are not responsible for mining projects, they bear the greatest burden of the negative environmental impacts. Curtis (2005) argues that while the price of gold dips from near-record levels on the world markets, poor people and communities in Obuasi in Ghana are suffering huge social and environmental costs and alleged human rights abuses as a result of gold mining. Large tracts of agricultural lands have been taken over for surface gold mining activities in communities across Africa.

In Ghana, communities such as Tarkwa, Prestea, Dumasi, Obuasi, Kenyasi, Chirano, Bibiani, Teleku-Bukaazo, Bolgatanga, Nadowli, Akwatia, and Adaa have lost large tracts of lands previously used for cultivation of various cash and food crops. Dozens of rivers and streams in these mining areas have been rendered unhealthy for drinking, fishing, recreation and watering of crops and livestock. A study by Akabzaa (2007) in Obuasi highlights how rivers and streams have been polluted with arsenic, iron, manganese and heavy metals from gold mining activities of AngloGold-Ashanti. The ESIA has been widely applied to mining projects and new monitoring and compliance instruments, such as concurrent reclamation and environmental performance rating and disclosure known as 'AKOBEN', has been introduced. However, challenges with the ESIA procedure have constrained governance for environmental protection. These challenges include: the low level of involvement of some actors, especially local communities and small-scale miners (Darimani, 2011); the inadequacy and poor timeliness of public notification; the lack of benchmarks for participation and feedback mechanisms; inadequate technical capacity of communities to comprehend EIA reports, and; the dominance of powerful individuals or groups at public hearings. Therefore, although the ESIA may technically comply with all the required procedures, it may still not adequately address many of the environmental and social concerns of mining, let alone redistribute the environmental burdens proportionately.

Inequality and discrimination in the distribution of benefits also appear among actors within communities in mining areas. In a study of the effectiveness of environmental governance in the Obuasi and Birim North Districts of Ghana, Darimani (2011) observed that benefits of environmental governance outcomes occur differently in different localities, according to different social and gender variables (Table 4.5). On a scale of 1 to 7, Darimani ranked a number of outcome variables for selected social and interest groups - chiefs, adult men, adult women, tenant farmers, District Assembly members, village committee members, and youth. This was done at focus group discussions in Binsere and Dokyiwaa in the Obuasi municipality and Addausena and Yayaaso in Birim North District.

Table 4. 5 Scale of benefits of environmental governance outcomes to different groups

Groups	Social structures	Voice in decision-making	Support for livelihood enhancement projects	Compliance with agreed decisions and local values	Reduced incidence of conflicts and tension	Acquisition of new skills for resource management	Uninterrupted access to environmental-resources
Chiefs	7	7	7	5	4	2	5
Adult men	3	6	4	7	5	5	4
Adult women	4	2	5	4	7	6	7
Tenant farmers	1	1	2	3	2	4	3
Assembly members	6	5	1	2	3	1	2
Committee members	2	4	6	1	2	3	1
Youth	5	3	3	6	6	7	6

Source: (Darimani, 2011)

On the scale, 1 means 'least' benefits, 2 is 'very low' benefits, 3 means 'low' benefits, 4 is for 'average' benefits; 5 for 'above average' benefits, 6 means 'high' benefits, and 7 is for 'very high' benefits. At each focus group discussion, participants were asked to indicate on the scale how they perceived the benefits from mining for the different social interest groups. The responses for each outcome were aggregated and ranked for the different social interest groups, as shown in Table 4.5. For the outcome relating to 'voice in decision-making', chiefs scored 'very high' benefits and tenant farmers scored the 'least' benefits (Darimani, 2011). While the outcomes in the Table are social, they illustrate a disproportionate distribution of benefits among actors.

Conclusion and recommendations

The analysis in this chapter indicates that state policies for the mining sector is discriminatory in favour of actors who hold power or are proximate to power. The mining policy regime in Ghana has prioritised the interest of transnational capital over all other interests, including the need to optimise the benefits of mining for the country and its population. Transnational investors in extractive industries have been and remain the major beneficiaries of mining in Ghana, while the politically weak actors - ordinary community persons, settler farmers and women - benefit the least, although they are the ones most affected by the negative environmental impacts of mining. The inequality in the distribution of the mineral wealth, the destruction of livelihoods and the environment, and the dispossession of land and water resources all clearly illustrates the fact that despite the presence and ascent of collaborative governance in mining, it has contributed only modestly in balancing the scale of power and in enhancing equitable distribution and management of the mineral wealth. Governance in the mining areas has not made any significant contributions to protecting the environment and to equitable distribution of the burden of environmental degradation caused by mining. For most ordinary people in communities affected by mining, governance initiatives undertaken by mining companies are simply a dramatic display, involving techniques of impression and credibility management. This chapter recommends that to truly enhance the equitable distribution and management of the wealth of mining through sound environmental management in Africa, action be taken the following policy recommendations.

A fundamental prerequisite for enhancing the equitable distribution and management of mineral resources in Africa through sound environmental management is to rebalance the scales of power of control and domination. This would be a starting point for an important shift in the character of state mining and environment policies. Efforts should be made to break from the current enclave production and shift towards a mining regime that fosters sustainable development, with increased linkages, value-addition and a fiscal mining regime that is fair and transparent and that optimises revenue collection and distribution.

Thus, it is recommended that the incentive packages granted to mining companies be reviewed. In Ghana, this package was devised at a time that government really needed to induce transnational capital into the mining sector. Inducing investment should not remain the focus of state policy forever. As part of the review, stabilisation as a legal provision should be abolished. Stabilisation has a locking effect as it does not allow government the flexibility to adjust taxes as and when necessary. Also, windfall tax (additional profit tax) should also be introduced, capital allowance brought down to about 20 per cent instead of the current 80 per cent initially and 50 per cent subsequently.

The portion of mineral royalties that goes to the local government should also be stepped up, consistent with the vision of decentralisation and aligned with the current model of composite budgeting. In addition, guidelines should be developed for the utilisation of the portions of royalty payments to the chiefs and traditional councils in ways that are aligned with the development agenda of the traditional area and district as a whole. If a chief happens to be both the occupant of the stool and head of the traditional council, the royalty payable to that chief is very close to amount received by the District Assembly. Yet, while there are rules of procedure for public accountability for the Assembly, these rules of procedure do not apply to chiefs.

Improved participation in decision-making, from project inception through to production, distribution and utilisation of the mineral wealth, as well as more accountability of public institutions and

97

mining companies, are important requirements for enhanced collaboration. While the ESIA has been widely applied to mining projects as a participatory environmental management tool, effective participation has been limited to mere technical compliance of organising public forums and meetings. Addressing this inadequacy requires clear minimum benchmarks for participation, especially for communities that will be affected by the mine.

To control the erratic declaration of dividends and to increase dividend payments to government, the discretionary powers of mining companies should be curtailed. To achieve this, government should negotiate and/or legislate a fixed percentage of revenue at which companies must declare dividends. A fixed percentage has the advantage of providing government with a framework for predictable revenue for budgetary planning. In addition, government has the opportunity to use the declaration of dividends as an incentive tool; the more regularly and consistently that a company declares dividends the more that it may qualify for some type of concessions. But such concessionary rewards should not outweigh dividend receipts.

Effective coordination among mining and environment sector institutions is recommended to ensure and promote information exchange, efficiency, joint monitoring and compliance enforcement. With respect to revenue, the Minerals Commission, Ghana Revenue Authority and Bank of Ghana may need to establish clear and timely channels of information on payments, receipts and utilisation of mineral revenue. They also need to track trends at the global level to help in determining certain taxes on an annual basis. Similar communication arrangements are required between the Environmental Protection Agency and the Inspectorate Division of the Minerals Commission, especially with respect to environmental monitoring and compliance enforcement.

Central government structures must cede to the local level, Metropolitan, Municipal and District Assemblies, greater involvement and authority in the granting of mineral rights, as well as of environmental and operating permits. Currently, most of the Assemblies have simply been reduced to arenas of posting notices and holding public hearings. One area in which a clear mandate could be defined for the Assemblies is that of resettlement and relocation. Currently, there are no guidelines for resettlement of villages displaced by mining operations.

Finally, there is often the tendency for governance to focus on the narrow specific interest of participating actors. The result has tended to undermine the attainment of collective interest, particularly of the environment. Therefore, the role of governance should constantly seek to harmonise the individual interests of actors with the collective interest.

References

Akabzaa, M. T. 2000. Boom and dislocation environmental and social impacts of mining in the Wassa West District of the Western Region of Ghana. Accra: Third Network-Africa.

Akabzaa, M.T. 2007. The glittering facade effects of mining activities on Obuasi and its surrounding communities. Accra: Third World Network, Africa.

Akabzaa, M. T. 2009. Mining in Ghana: Implications for national economic development and poverty reduction. In: Campbell, B. (ed.) Mining in Africa, regulation and development New York: Pluto Press, Ottawa: International Development Research Centre, and Uppsala: Nordiska Afrikainstitutet.

Ansell, C. and Gash, A. 2007. Collaborative governance in theory and practice. Journal of Public Administration Research and Theory 18, 543–571.

Aryee, J., Søreide, T., Shukla, G. P. and Minh, L. T. 2011. Political economy of the mining sector in Ghana. Policy Research Working Paper. The World Bank Africa Region Public Sector Reform and Capacity-building Unit.

Campbell, B. (ed.) 2004. Regulating mining in Africa: for whose benefit? Uppsala: Nordiska Afrika Institutet.

Cleaver, F. and Franks, T. 2005. Water governance and poverty: A framework for analysis. BCID Research Paper. Bradford Centre for International Development, University of Bradford.

Commission on Human Rights and Administrative Justice. 2008. The state of human rights in mining communities in Ghana. Accra: CHRAJ.

Curtis, M. 2005. Gold rush: The impact of gold mining on poor people in Obuasi in Ghana. London: Action Aid.

Darimani, A. 2011. Effective environmental governance of gold mining in Obuasi and Birim North Districts of Ghana. Accra: University of Ghana.

Dwivedi, O. P. 2002. On common good and good governance: An alternative approach. Bloomfield, CT: Kumarian Press Inc.

ECA. 2007. Report of the Big Table conference. Addis Ababa, Ethiopia: United Nations Economic Commission for Africa.

Graham, J., Amos, B. and Plumptre, T. 2003. Governance principles for protected areas in the 21st Century: A discussion paper. Ottawa, Canada: Institute on Governance.

Hamdok, A. 2003. Governance and policy in Africa: Recent experiences. In: Kayizzi-Mugerwa (ed.) Reforming Africa's institutions. Tokyo and New York: United Nations University Press.

Hyden, G. and Court, J. 2002. Comparing governance across countries and over time: Conceptual challenges. In: Dele, O. and Soumana, S. (eds.) Better governance and public policy. Bloomfield, CT: Kumarian Press Inc.

Minerals Commission of Ghana. 2004. Statistical overview of Ghana's mineral industry 2003. Accra: Report, Finance, Marketing and Research Department.

Minerals Commission of Ghana. 2009. Minerals concessions map of Ghana.

MSSP. 2011. Final evaluation of mining sector support programme, Final report. November 2011. Accra: Mining Sector Support Programme (MSSP)

Republic of Ghana 2006. Minerals and Mining Act, Act 703. Accra, Ghana.

World Bank. 2006. Where is the wealth of nations? Measuring capital for the XXI century. Washington, DC: The World Bank.

United Nations Conference on Trade and Development (UNCTAD). 2005. Economic development in Africa: Rethinking the role of foreign direct investment. New York and Geneva: United Nations.

Zadek, S. 2006. The logic of collaborative governance: Corporate responsibility, accountability and the social contract. Corporate Social Responsibility Initiative Working Paper No. 17. Cambridge, MA: John F. Kennedy School of Government, Harvard University.

Chapter Five

Labour 'Specialisation' and Sustenance of Artisanal Mining Activity in Ghana

Frank K. Nyame[5]

Introduction

Artisanal mining of gold and diamonds has gained prominence throughout Sub-Saharan Africa and in many parts of the world, especially in resource-rich developing countries with high unemployment, low per capita income and limited economic opportunities for many poor people. In Ghana, estimates of the number of people involved, the annual production from the artisanal small-scale (ASM) mines and their overall contribution to the national economy vary due to the generally unregulated, informal and often seasonal nature of ASM activity (Aryee et al., 2003, Hilson and Potter, 2003, Aubynn, 2006). Just as in other countries where ASM is extensive, studies in Ghana have documented some form of 'labour differentiation or specialisation' at many sites, apparently related to gender (male and female) or age (i.e. children and adults) with regard to specific activities the different groups performed (MacDonald, 2006, Yakovleva, 2007). It is, however, becoming increasingly evident that specialisation of labour in the ASM sector may have evolved from the recognisably 'simple classification' above, into one that is far more complex and highly dynamic than previously envisaged. Jaques et al. (2006) reported the presence of well-defined structures and high degrees of organisation, typically resembling those of a small mine, at ASM sites in Burkina Faso. This is particularly the case for male miners, compared with female participants in mining operations.

---

[5] Lecturer, Department of Earth Science, University of Ghana, Legon-Accra, Ghana

In the current study, for instance, groups of people were encountered that moved from place to place in search of new or potential mineral deposits, in a process they describe as 'testing' (i.e. exploration). Others, however, confine themselves to extraction or mining of ore (digging) at specific sites, haulage and processing (i.e. washing) or beneficiation of ore. Some mainly engage in mine-support services, such as the provision of tools and equipment including spare parts, recruitment of labour, sale of medicines, provision of credit and attending to the spiritual needs of miners. Many of these miners or mining groups perform specific or specialised tasks either individually for a fee or as part of a group in the overall production or supply chain of gold and diamonds, which are the two most important commodities from Ghana's artisanal mining sector.

Thus, even though the well-documented rudimentary, labour intensive, low skilled, equipment-starved ASM operations still prevail (Aryee et al., 2003, Hentschel et al., 2003), there is evidence to suggest that increasingly, ASM operations are incorporating some degree of 'sophistication' and specialisation. This involves the introduction of various skills, equipment and distinct processes of operations that have led to increased output. To date, however, the link between specialisation (or differentiation) of labour and artisanal mining activity has not been studied in detail so there has been inadequate knowledge of the changing nature of the tasks performed by various groups at mine sites, and their relative contributions to ASM productivity.

This chapter explores the impact of labour specialisation in the largely informal but socio-economically important ASM sector. In this study, labour specialisation refers to the differentiation of labour/services or distinct processes performed for fairly long periods of time by artisanal miners or groups at their sites of operation. In this context, the term specialisation is used synonymously with differentiation and/or division of labour.

Study area and methods

The study documented in this chapter was undertaken in Ghana between 2007 and 2011 at many active ASM sites and communities, including the Wassa Amenfi West District, Western Region (Dominase, Agona Amenfi, Kwabeng, Gyedua Kese,

103

Asankran Breman), Wassa Amenfi East District, Western Region (Jappa, Nanankaw), Komenda-Edina-Eguafo-Abirem District, Central Region (Abirem Eguafo and surrounding areas), Upper Denkyira District (Ayamfuri), Akwatia and surrounding areas (Eastern Region), and Dokrupe and Kuii (Northern Region). Experience from earlier research work on various aspects of artisanal mining showed that many miners, mining groups and communities tend to be suspicious or sceptical of researchers' motives and especially apprehensive of formal questionnaire administration techniques. This is probably because artisanal mining activity is largely informal or illegal. Additionally, miners spoke of research fatigue. For these reasons, this study used data gathered mainly from in-person informal interviews and interactions with participants at mine sites and within communities where artisanal mining is actively undertaken. With this approach, miners freely participated in the interactions and willingly provided information, especially relating to specialised labour and services. In addition, observations at several sites where mining was in progress also proved very useful.

The mining industry and ASM activity in Ghana

Until the 1980s, the mining industry landscape in Ghana was dominated by large-scale mines (LSMs), mainly transnational companies that exploited gold, diamonds, bauxite and manganese in mineral-rich areas of the country. Thereafter, various factors combined to produce a veritable explosion of the ASM sector, which saw increased numbers of people, mainly unemployed, who flooded the sector to try to eke out a living. The ASM sector, characterised by the environmental degradation it caused, its poor health and safety records and other socioeconomic vices associated with it, prompted many official attempts to regulate or mainstream ASM to formalise the activities of the miners. However, a combination of factors have over time spawned a vibrant ASM sector, especially for gold mining, which now effectively rivals LSM companies in terms of production and intensity of activity. These factors include internal or local ones in Ghana such as rapid population growth, increasing unemployment, less meaningful growth in the national economy, and institutional weaknesses. There have also been external or global factors at play, including rising and falling commodity prices, structural adjustment programmes, improved technology in the mining industry and restructuring in the LSM share of the mining economy. Efforts by governments through the promulgation of laws (e.g. PNDC Laws 153 and 218; Mining and minerals Act, 2006) and the establishment of regulatory institutions (e.g. Minerals Commission and Precious Minerals Marketing Company) to mainstream or formalise the sector have, thus far, not achieved much success. Over the past few decades, therefore, ASM has become synonymous with an informal mining economy dominated by both Ghanaians and migrants, mostly from the West African sub-region, which operates largely outside governmental control.

'Specialised' labour and services in ASM

As noted above, the ASM sector in Ghana has been evolving from what was originally a rudimentary, localised, apparently disorganised, 'sedentary', predominantly unskilled and seasonally-oriented activity, to one that is sophisticated, widespread, much more organised, migratory, semi-skilled or quite skilled, and a semi-permanent or even permanent, an activity that people of various trades and/or nationalities undertake in many parts of the mineral-rich country. One direct consequence of this transformation has been the advent and/or incorporation of fairly distinct forms of labour and services as integral components of ASM operations. This usually involves people who form an integral part of the mining group, with shares in the ultimate profit. But others that are deeply involved are people outside the mining group whose sole interest and remuneration depend on their ability to perform specific tasks over a period of time, reminiscent of sub-contracting in the LSM segment of the mining economy. Specialisation can be observed in all the major stages of exploration, extraction, transportation and processing of ore-bearing material.

Exploration

A few decades ago, the search for mineral deposits for ASM was primarily undertaken by a few artisanal miners that often drew on local knowledge to locate pre-existing or old mine sites for sampling before deciding whether or not to mine in a given area. Currently, however, exploration may be not only an important first step but an essential component of ASM activity, where people prospect for and then trade potential mine sites to prospective miners. Exploration teams of two or more people have often been encountered in the field whose role is to explore or, in their parlance, 'test places' on behalf of mining groups or sponsors of ASM activities. One such group of active artisanal mining 'explorers' was encountered in the Manso Nkran area in the Ashanti Region in November 2008. According to them, they were searching for new mining areas for a fee for local investors or sponsors of artisanal mining. Other groups constitute distinct teams within mining groups whose sole responsibility is to prospect for favourable ground. Interactions with some ASM exploration teams indicate that many had previously worked in large-scale mining or exploration companies. There they acquired some experience in rock, soil and sediment sampling techniques and this equipped them with the requisite know-how to explore or prospect for minerals for ASM.

The major difference observed between ASM and LSM exploration teams is that the former rarely, if ever, take samples to recognised laboratories for analysis. ASM explorers usually rely on visual inspection, limited processing of suspected ore material (rock, soil or sediment), manual pulverisation and amalgamation, or the addition of mercury for qualitative interpretation and subsequent decisions about whether to mine or not. One member in a group of three that was actively chiselling in a pit in the Nanankaw area in western Ghana explained as follows;

'I worked with an exploration company that came to Asuowin in the Ashanti Region. At first we were employed as labourers to show them where the old mines that the white men used to work were located. When we went to those places, they saw the big machines, many pits and tunnels in the bush. Galamsey people were already working there. They took samples from the soil and rocks and we carried them to the camp. When they entered pits and adits and took samples of the stones, we saw which parts of the stone they took and which parts they did not take. "Sometimes we ask them and they will tell us which stone is good and which [stone] is not good". After they stayed for about six months, we became very free with the technicians and sometimes they make us take [rock and soil samples] while they looked on. If you are good to the technicians, they could show you how to take samples. Even

106

in the tunnels they could make us use chisel to take some stones. So after they left, we also used that to test some places. We take the samples and grind and if you see gold, then that place is good. Sometimes we also add "med" [mercury]. In the past four years, we got six good places for mining, five for dig and wash [alluvial] and one rock [hard or weathered rock material].'

Ore extraction

The bulk of specialised labour activities are associated with the extraction of ore-bearing rock. Irrespective of the nature of the material, whether it is alluvial or hard rock (primary or weathered), the traditional ASM methods - manual, physically tasking 'pick and shovel' excavation - are gradually being replaced by a variety of earth-moving or loosening equipment. The equipment allows ASM miners to remove greater volumes of ore material in a given period of time. In general, the high waste-to-ore ratio closer to the surface means that huge volumes of un-mineralised rock or soil have to be excavated to access ore-bearing rock at various depths below the surface.

In hard-rock ASM mining, specialised activities such as sinking and timbering of shafts, pitting and tunnelling, drilling and blasting, chiselling and hoisting of ore or waste from shafts are typically undertaken by people with the requisite skills, knowledge or experience. People with such specialised skills are mostly contracted specifically for jobs and may not form part of the mining group. During the study, some were observed moving from one mine site to another to provide services to mainly artisanal mining groups in drilling, blasting, maintenance of worn-out equipment and dewatering of pits and shafts using low horse-power pumps. From the ASM alluvial diamond fields of Akwatia in eastern Ghana, to ASM hard-rock shaft-mining at Grupe in northern Ghana, these specialised services enabled miners to increase production substantially. At one site in this study, miners showed us two heaps of ore-bearing material, one a small heap excavated using chisels and shovels and the other a huge heap done more recently with the help of 'contractors' using drilling and blasting (pneumatolitic) equipment. Apparently suspicious of our motives, they declined to give information on the source and cost of hiring out the equipment to miners per day by sponsors or investors.

Ore transport, processing and marketing

Unlike a decade ago when ore from points of extraction to processing sites was mainly head-ported, an activity done mostly by women and children, today the bulk of extracted ore is increasingly being transported by hired contractors using light- to heavy-duty vehicles. Such contractors are usually paid according to the number of hours worked, trips made and, in some cases, 'measurable' loads carted per day. However, because vehicles do not easily gain access to ore extraction sites, head-porting of materials from pits and from around shafts to places of conveyance by vehicles still constitutes a significant task, mostly undertaken by groups of women and children.

During processing, ore-bearing alluvial material is usually mixed with water and 'gravity separated' on a sluice or an inclined arrangement. For hard-rock material, whether weathered or fresh, the pre-processing treatment of grinding and milling to a fine particle size amenable to further treatment by sluicing and/or amalgamation, is now a very important intermediary process undertaken to liberate the ore metal from gangue or matrix of the host rock. Because gold mainly occurs in sub-microscopic grains in such rocks, the finer the degree of communition (process in which solid materials are reduced in size by crushing, grinding and other processes), the better the recovery of the ore. People with access to or experience with operating grinding and milling equipment are therefore either engaged or play a major role in processing such ore-bearing materials for ASMs.

To ensure constant processing and also to reduce idle machine time, independently operated 'centralised' processing facilities manned by skilled mechanics have been set up in proximity to some artisanal mine sites, and miners transport ore material to these sites for processing at a fee. At Tarkwa, Bawdie and Bogoso in western Ghana, such centralised milling sites continuously process ore material. Artisanal miners that patronise these services cite several advantages of such centralised processing, including efficiency and reliability, a constant source of power and also convenience. In addition, these central processing sites are seldom targeted by security and regulatory agencies because they are some distance from the ore-extracting ASM sites, which regulators tend to target.

Marketing of the produce from the ASMs, for example gold and diamonds, can be done by people directly involved in the mining process, middlemen or investors whose only interest is to purchase at mine sites (for a 'bush price') or at designated marketing centres in towns. A variety of tools or equipment, such as weighing scales, pincers and weights, are used to establish the market value of the gold or diamonds. Because market information can now be sourced via the internet or mobile phones, marketing of ASM produce is also fast becoming a separate activity that enables miners to maximise profits and improve on production.

Other ancillary or support services

Specialisation is also seen in the ancillary and support services both on and off mine sites and is important in the production, marketing and supply chain for gold and diamonds. For example, vendors of items and products in that supply chain, including mercury, spare parts, food, clothing and medicines, enter into various forms of symbiotic trading arrangements with miners, ranging from barter to cash payments. Others, such as traditional priests, play a very crucial role in the performance of rites at new or active ASMs. Their activities straddle all stages of the mine's life, from exploration, through mining and processing, to marketing.

Factors contributing to growth of specialised labour in ASM

Specialisation, the ability of individuals, businesses and countries to concentrate on specific products or tasks to be exchanged and traded for other goods or services (Lindbeck and Snower, 1997, Luthans, 1998), is an essential feature of many modern economic systems. Hitherto, specialisation was limited in scope, rare or unknown at many ASM sites in Ghana. It began to gain prominence a few decades ago probably as a result of a shift in ASM activity from dominantly subsistence to 'medium-scale, business-oriented' activity. As artisanal mining gained some degree of permanency, in terms of sites of operation and workforce, a kind of 'division of labour' emerged, ostensibly as the result of attempts to increase production and profitability.

Emergence of specialised labour can be attributed to global, national and local factors (mining community level), which serve to re-shape the artisanal sector and the mining industry as a whole. Global factors that have directly or indirectly played a major role in ASM labour specialisation include high commodity (especially gold) prices. These include an increased trade and information flow, the availability of simple but improved extraction and processing techniques, and a ready market for minerals as a result of the fairly substantial but 'informal' inflow of foreign capital into the sector. Observations at artisanal mine sites suggest such capital mainly comes in the form of mining and processing equipment as well as cash and are mainly provided by individuals and groups from China, India, Russia, Ukraine, Italy, USA and Canada. Today, the role of some people within a group of miners may be for them to stay in the nearest urban environment constantly monitor the daily average world market price of gold via the internet and then relay this information via cell phones to the mining sites. This marketing strategy ensures timely information on price fluctuations. Others, mainly foreigners (Chinese), deal in various kinds of processing equipment, which they either sell or lease to miners on hire purchase.

At the national level, industry-wide reforms, liberalised economic policies of governments from the 1980s and a weak-to-non-existent regulatory environment may have contributed to the rise of ASM activity in general (Aryee, 2001b, Hilson and Potter, 2003, Banchirigah, 2006) and, ultimately, to increased specialisation of labour into the production process. These may have been complemented by other 'pull' factors, such as increased population growth, improved telecommunications and road infrastructure, economically unattractive traditional subsistence agriculture, desire of the younger generation for 'quick' money (Nyame and Blocher, 2010), erratic and unpredictable weather conditions likely resulting from climate change, the ready market for metallic commodities such as gold, and low entry barriers into ASM.

Reforms in the mining sector and concomitant restructuring, together with advances in mining technology in the past few decades, have led to redundancies of a mainly low- to semi-skilled LSM workforce. Many of those who were laid off transited either as individuals or groups to artisanal mining where they put to use the knowledge and experience they had gained in LSM companies. In addition, the transfer of technology and skills, especially from mineral exploration and from foreign mining (exploration) companies that took up properties and worked for a time in the country, have also provided the necessary impetus for increased ASM activity. Cumulatively, these companies temporarily employed and trained many people in a wide range of skills, ranging from sampling and sample preparation, to processing and treatment of ore (e.g. alluvial material). When such companies departed or were dissolved, many semi-skilled people that had been earning relatively good incomes found themselves without employment and resorted to work in the ASM sector.

At the local level, the availability of low-grade but often abundant mineral resources has also played a significant role in the growth of ASMs and drawn many unemployed people, especially the youth, into artisanal mining as a source of livelihood. In addition, mining communities tend to serve as 'growth points' in rural, development-starved frontier areas of the country. In the past decade in Ghana, some artisanal mining communities have witnessed tremendous transformation from remote and inaccessible and/or small settlements into 'boom' villages and towns, local economies having qualitatively benefited directly from the inflow of investment, people and services. Information gathered during this study suggests that as a result of the direct benefits that they can personally derive from ASMs, some local or community leaders pursue an investment drive by aggressively encouraging and tacitly assisting prospective miners to explore and exploit minerals on their customary lands (Nyame and Blocher, 2010). If minerals are discovered in an area, this find then induces influxes of people with varied interests into the area, who perform different tasks but with the sole aim of profiting from the mine's presence. Communities such as Afiena and Gurumisa in the Wasa Amenfi Traditional area in western Ghana, for example, narrated how they still continue to actively pursue such an 'investment drive' in the hope of attracting artisanal miners to sites abandoned by colonial explorers in the first half of the last century.

111

Specialisation and sustenance of ASM activity

Labour specialisation (or differentiation), as posited in this study, significantly sustains artisanal mining by utilising, in a much more efficient manner, the various stages of ASM activity and thus results in substantially increased production and output (Figure 5.1). Although distinctly separate groups may be involved at any one time at an artisanal mining site, there is a convergence of interest towards a common, profit-oriented objective. Specialisation sustains artisanal mining through the 'traditional' factors of production, including access to mineral lands, capital and credit, availability of labour or skills and entrepreneurship development.

Figure 5. 1 Relationship between labour specialisation and sustenance of ASM activity

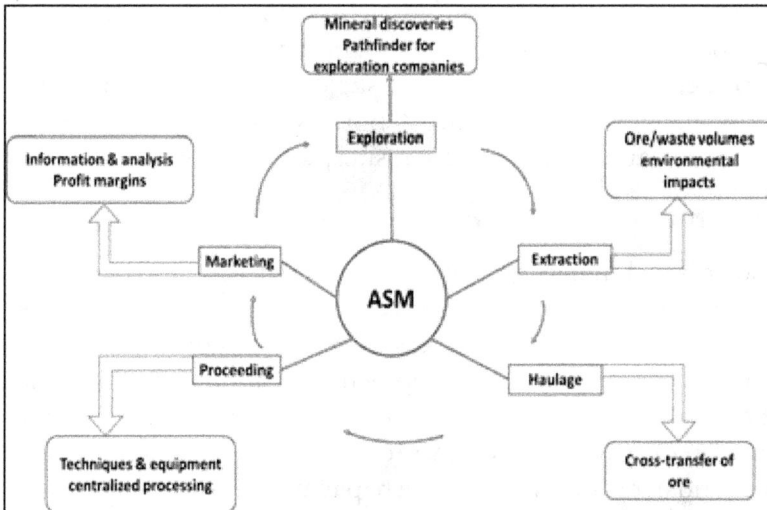

Access to land and mineral resources

Specialisation has created opportunities for artisanal - mainly illegal - miners to fairly easily access mineral-rich lands, an important requisite for ASM activity. 'Land scouters', who are often part of or precede an exploration team, visit communities to negotiate on behalf of or to trade and/or partner with potential miners, mining groups or sponsors (investors) and thereby gain access to land for the eventual exploitation of mineral deposits. In a sense, this is similar to tenement departments in LSM companies. This has been partly aided by customary land tenure practices (Nyame and Blocher (2010), weak monitoring and enforcement of existing mining laws. Due to the mutually beneficial relationship between miners and customary land-owners, who predominantly control mineral-rich lands in Ghana, miners readily gain access to land through various customary tenancy arrangements. This has led to increased discoveries of gold deposits in many parts of the country that are not economically viable for LSM, but that have, in turn, provided many unemployed people with livelihoods.[6]

However, because no formal contractual agreements are made between miners and host communities or land-owners, breaches often occur on both sides that engender social conflicts between miners and local people. At Gyedua Kese in the Amenfi West District, for example, traditional landowners alleged that miners absconded without fulfilling promises of payment, which had been agreed upon before start of their operations on customary lands given to them. In this instance, investigations indicated that many local people, including women porters and vehicle owners contracted to cart ore to processing sites, were left unpaid.

Availability of capital and credit

Because artisanal miners generally lack access to credit from formal lending institutions, the roles of investors, middlemen or sponsors become very crucial in the success of their operations. Capital in the form of various types of equipment and funds are channelled into the ASM sector by both local and foreign investors who have filled the credit gap. They often provide credit either against gold (or diamonds) produced or as cash payments on various terms. Commonly, capital is often in the form of processing equipment, such as mechanical diggers or excavators, loaders, bulldozers and 'Chang Fa', a typical brand name for equipment mainly sourced

---

[6] In just one year (in 2009), three new hard-rock-mining sites opened near Dominase and Agona in the Wassa Amenfi West District in Ghana's Western Region. Except for old native pits that dotted the alluvial landscape, this area was previously unknown for hard-rock gold mineralisation. A visit to one mine site revealed that the miners had traced a quartz vein in Birimian phyllite, observable on a farm track and subsequently opened a huge pit just about 10 metres from the outcropping vein.

from China, all of which have replaced the hammer and chisel as tools for the extraction and 'communition' of rocks. By law, the ASM sector is reserved for Ghanaians, but some local people, for want of capital or to attract investment, front for foreign entrepreneurs who bring in equipment for mining.

The introduction of mechanised equipment for mining, together with new processing technology and the ready availability of mercury, have led to increased volumes of material being extracted and processed and thus an increased output. Estimated figures available at the Minerals Commission suggest that ASM activity has consistently produced significant amounts of gold and diamonds for the past several years, an observation which may well coincide with increased specialisation of ASM operations.

Some national and transnational migrants also invest money into the ASM business for production and marketing to avoid passing through the formal regulatory or financial (e.g. banking) regime. This practice which may lead to money laundering, encourage smuggling of minerals out of the country and, invariably, result in the net loss of revenue to the nation.

Advances in communications and technology infrastructure, together with improved road networks in the country, have enhanced the exchange of information among ASM operators involved in the sector, from exploration through to mining and marketing of gold and diamonds.[7] These advances, in turn, enable people to effectively render specialised services to the ASM sub-economy in various ways. Apart from miners, sponsors and other interested people offer diverse forms of investment services at agreeable fees payable either in monetary terms or by barter in the form of gold or diamonds. Sub-contracting services are also available through many informal arrangements and agreements.

---

[7] At a recent (April 2011) ASM site at Kwabeng in the Wassa Amenfi West district, after initial testing by an exploration team, within just one month excavators and other equipment and thousands of people were already assembled at the site. Just a decade ago, such a site could not have been so active within such a short period.

114

Labour and skills

Typical or stereotypic artisanal mining is generally synonymous with rudimentary tools, low capital, low skill levels and little input in terms of equipment used, and a lack of sophistication. In the traditional ASMs, women, children and old people generally undertook jobs seen as 'light' and less physically challenging, while younger able-bodied men engaged in more demanding, multi-tasking and exhausting jobs.

With increasing specialisation, however, jobs undertaken by miners not only become more defined and repetitive but are also determined and/or measured by output, with remuneration often commensurate with the job done per given period of time. This has, for example, enabled many retired or retrenched LSM personnel to find an 'economic lifeline' in ASM activity through provision of essential services such as sinking and timbering of shafts and blasting of rocks that enable miners to increase production and work in fairly safe conditions compared with those of previous decades. At Prestea in western Ghana, semi-skilled, former mine personnel such as mine captains or assistants, blast men and shift bosses, have all been engaged at ASM sites. Where there is apparent conflict over land use or resources, well-built and strong young men or 'macho men' as they are known, play crucial roles at mine sites to guard against trespassing and to protect the mining interests of individuals, communities or investors in the ASM sector.

ASM is also becoming less seasonal. Formerly, it tended to be very brisk in the dry season, while mining activities were curtailed during the rainy season when streams, river valleys or pits and shafts were flooded. Although there is still less mining activity in the rainy season, specialisation of ASM permits more mining to be undertaken year round. Miners can fairly easily switch from alluvial mining in the rainy season to hard-rock-mining in the dry season or else work throughout the year by using powerful water pumps, grinding and earth-moving equipment to work hard-rock deposits.

Some aspects of gender-related labour specialisation are also observed. In the diamond fields of Akwatia in eastern Ghana, female miners or mine owners interviewed confirmed that they cede activities such as final processing or sorting of diamonds and

115

roasting of amalgam (mercury-gold mixture) to their husbands or trusted representatives. Information gathered suggested that women and children are usually excluded in these final operations due to certain socio-cultural beliefs, for example, that gold may 'vanish' when women are involved in the final processing. Such practices, even though gender-biased and/or discriminatory, may be practically good for the health of women since they may not be predisposed to working long hours in stagnant pools of water or exposed to dangerous chemicals that might be injurious to their health.

In Ghana, many new artisanal mining sites have been opened in the past few years. One such site at Eguafo Ebirem (near the coastal town of Elmina in central Ghana) was opened in early 2011 by artisanal miners who hail from the area but who were, for a very long time, part of a group of miners in the Tarkwa mining district in western Ghana. In the Akwatia area in eastern Ghana, groups of 'migrating or mobile diggers with their tools of trade' were encountered soliciting for contract jobs from one mine site to another. According to them, being constantly on the move enables them to easily find jobs.

Traditional healers and medicine men, some of whom move with migrating miners, take care of the socio-cultural, spiritual and mental health needs of miners. Similar strong influences of 'earth priests' have been reported in artisanal mining communities in Burkina Faso (Luning, 2006). According to miners interviewed, the healers provide protection against calamities and also ensure success in mining operations. Because of their services, miners are encouraged as well as emboldened to undertake risky jobs and to be hopeful of good returns on their operations. One important aspect of the involvement of traditional healers in mining teams concerns community entry practices. For example, mining groups accompanied by healers or medicine men bond fairly easily with host communities, and their presence also facilitates entry of miners into those communities. This may be due to similarities in culture and belief systems between miners and local communities as well as reverence for such traditional medicine men in Ghanaian societies.

Specialisation has also contributed to the accelerated migration of miners and mining groups, both internally in Ghana and within the sub-region, on a much larger scale than previously existed in the ASM sector. As people get more skills and specialise, they are encouraged to further move to other mine sites in various parts of the country or across national borders to other countries within the sub-region to take advantage of new opportunities. The existence of a mobile, semi-skilled labour force that can easily move from one mine site to the other to perform various tasks has greatly influenced the way in which artisanal mining takes place. For example, Ghanaian artisanal miners are now known to operate in Burkina Faso, Benin, Sierra Leone and Liberia.

At an ASM site near Tarkwa in western Ghana, a migrant traditional healer not specifically linked to any mining group recounted having served various clients in the vicinity of Adamus Resources Limited's LSM property in the Nzema area (western Ghana), as well as groups of artisanal miners in the Nanankaw, Asankrangwa and Bibiani areas (western Ghana), and Bontefufuo area (Ashanti region). According to the healer, he was always on the move to execute periodic contracts and perform rites to ensure successful opening and continued operations of new mine sites.

Entrepreneurship and 'growth' in local mining communities

Entrepreneurship development seems to be on the rise as a result of specialisation in ASM activities. Many local entrepreneurs, both male and female and some with little or no prior knowledge of mining, are now investing time, effort and money in various aspects of the business or related services for a share of the eventual profits. Artisans and craftsmen, for example, produce locally made tools for replacement of worn-out equipment. Some also trade in goods and services essential for the upkeep of entire mining operations.

Most mining communities appear unanimous in their reception to ASM activity due to the direct benefits and especially socioeconomic 'security' that it brings to the local people. Some people even cite reduction in petty crime as an asset that ASM activity offers in local communities. Interviewed in February 2010, one village elder at Hiawa in the Wassa Amenfi West district of Ghana put it this way:

117

'Some of our youth who learnt trades in fitting (mechanics) and auto-electricians work with the miners, get some income and provide the needs of their families. In the cities, there are no jobs and they also don't have any place to stay. But over here they can work for themselves; some have their own farms, do "galamsey" [mainly illegal ASM activity] and also help with family issues. Because of the "galamsey", stealing has reduced in the town because young people can now get some work to do.'

Impact on mineral resources governance, environment, human trafficking, health and safety

Because labour specialisation in ASM has not been studied in detail in Ghana, its overall impact on governance in the mineral resources sector is largely unknown, especially since artisanal mining activity is still predominantly informal (or illegal). As indicated above, the artisanal mining sector, as illustrated by the numerous operational sites of miners in the country, now provides very strong 'indications or pathfinder information' for deposit occurrences in an area. Such information has been extensively utilised by LSM companies, many of which acquire mineral properties in areas of active (illegal) artisanal mining due to the likelihood that they are rich in minerals. Even though this may help reduce overall exploration costs and increase mineral discoveries in many parts of the country, the trend towards increased specialisation of activities in the largely informal mining sector may directly conflict and undermine the statutory regime on the granting of mining concessions and mineral rights.

Qualitatively, specialisation appears to have resulted in increased impacts on various aspects of the environment, miners and local communities. As a result of specialisation in exploration work, mining sites have not only increased but are also widely spread out throughout Ghana, exacting enormous pressure and taking a heavy toll on environmental resources, including vegetation, soils, streams and rivers. Human-trafficking, particularly of women, is also on the increase. With the high rates of unemployment, especially in rural mineral-rich areas and limited economic opportunities, many unemployed youth - both male and female - are easily lured to mine sites throughout the country and often find themselves working under deplorable conditions. Some get

118

trapped without the means to return to their places of origin. Others work for long hours in apparently unsafe working conditions such as in narrow, dark, air-vitiated pits several metres below the ground or topographic surface. In 2010, there were fatalities caused by collapse of an artisanal mining pit near Wasa Akropong in the Wassa Amenfi East district of the Western Region, and the victims were mostly women migrants that had been apparently trafficked to work in the mines. A report in the Ghanaian Times Newspaper of April 16, 2013 on seventeen illegal gold miners (galamsey operators) who unfortunately met their untimely death when the pit in which they were operating caved in at Kyekyewere in the Upper Denkyira East Municipality of the Central Region serves to illustrate the often risky and unsafe nature of many artisanal mining activities in Ghana.

Before specialisation, many miners frequently changed jobs within short periods of time at mine sites. With specialisation, however, miners constantly undertake routine and repetitive jobs for longer periods of time, making them more vulnerable to hazards such as noise, dust and mercury pollution. For example, miners who undertake continuous extraction of ore inside narrow, vitiated, dust-laden shafts will obviously be at a higher risk for and more prone to respiratory diseases than those who operate excavators or other mining equipment on the surface. In the same way, miners engaged in ore grinding and processing on the surface were more likely to be afflicted by inhalation of dust than those involved in ore haulage using trucks.

At some mine sites, distinctly separate groups or 'gangs' of people were observed to be responsible for grinding of ore and for roasting of amalgam (mercury-gold mixture) on open fires to recover gold. Without any protective gear whatsoever, people involved in ore grinding were found to be highly likely to suffer from continued dust inhalation, whereas roasting of amalgam will make those people more vulnerable to poisoning from over-exposure to and inhalation of mercury vapour.

Conclusion

Labour specialisation in the artisanal mining sector, though not a new phenomenon, has gained prominence as a result of both local and external factors, including high commodity prices, availability of simple but improved extraction and processing techniques, industry-wide restructuring, a weak regulatory regime, the abundance of low-grade ore material and inflow of investment into the sector from mainly informal sources. From exploration through extraction and processing of ore-bearing materials, specialisation has resulted in increased output, suggesting that ASM activity is progressing towards the path of a 'mature' economic undertaking. Increased specialisation and mechanisation of ASM production has led to increased environmental degradation, suggesting strongly that in spite of sustaining the sector, the risks and hazards associated with specialisation of artisanal mining activities cannot be ignored. The overall effect on weak governance of the mineral resources sector, health and safety of miners and communities is also of concern. Activities such as drilling and blasting of ore-bearing rock undertaken by people with little or no training in the use of explosives and detonators may ultimately pose serious risks to the overall health of miners and communities. Finally, various aspects of labour specialisation may run counter to statutory and development partners' arrangements that seek to regulate the ASM sector in the country.

References

Aryee, B. N. 2001b. Small-scale mining in Ghana as a sustainable development activity: its development and a review of the contemporary issues and challenges. In: Hilson, G. M. (ed.) Small-scale mining, rural subsistence and poverty in West Africa. Bourton-on-Dunsmore, UK: Practical Action Publishing.

Aryee, B. N. A., Ntibery, B. K. and Atorkui, E. 2003. Trends in the small-scale mining of precious minerals in Ghana: a perspective on its environmental impact. Journal of Cleaner Production 11, 131–140.

Aubynn, A. K. 2006. Live and let live: the relationship between artisanal/small-scale and large-scale miners at Abosso Goldfields, Ghana. In: Hilson, G. M. (ed.) Small-scale mining, rural subsistence and poverty in West Africa. Bourton-on Dunsmore, UK: Practical Action Publishing.

Banchirigah, S. M. 2006. How have reforms fuelled the expansion of artisanal mining? Evidence from Sub-Saharan Africa. Resources Policy 31(3): 165–171.

Ghanaian Times, April 16, 2013. 17 'galamseyers' buried in pit. http://www.ghheadlines.com/agency/Ghanaian-times/ 20130416

Hentschel, T., Hruschka, F. and Priester, M. 2003. Artisanal and small-scale mining: Challenges and opportunities. London: International Institute for Environment and Development (IIED).

Hilson, G. and Potter, C. 2003. Why is illegal gold mining so ubiquitous throughout rural Ghana? African Development Review 15, 237–270.

Jaques, E., Zida, B., Billa, M., Greffe, C. and Thormassin, J. 2006. Artisanal and small-scale gold mines in Burkina Faso: Today and tomorrow. In: HILSON, G. M. (ed.) Small-scale mining, rural subsistence and poverty in West Africa. UK: Practical Action Publishing.

Lindbeck, A. and Snower, D. J. 1997. The division of labour within firms. Stockholm, Sweden: Institute for International Economic Studies, University of Stockholm.

Luning, S. 2006. Artisanal gold mining in Burkina Faso: permits, poverty and perceptions of the poor in Sanmatenga, the 'land of gold'. In: HILSON, G. M. (ed.). Small-scale mining, rural subsistence and poverty in West Africa. Bourton-on-Dunsmore, UK: Practical Action Publishing.

Luthans, F. 1998. Organisational Behavior. Boston, MA: Irwin McGraw-Hill.

Macdonald, K. 2006. Artisanal and small-scale mining in West Africa: achieving sustainable development through environmental and human rights law. In: HILSON, G. M. (ed.) Small-scale mining, rural subsistence and poverty in West Africa. Bourton-on-Dunsmore, UK: Practical Action Publishing.

Nyame, F. K. and Blocher, J. 2010. Influence of land tenure practices on artisanal mining activity in Ghana. Resources Policy 35, 47–53.

Yakovleva, N. 2007. Perspectives on female participation in artisanal and small-scale mining: A case study of Birim North District of Ghana. Resources Policy 32(1–2), 29–41.

Chapter Six

Whither Sustainable Small and Medium Scale Mining in Guyana?

Paulette Bynoe[8]

Demystifying sustainability and sustainable mining

Mining has often been attributed a central role in the economic growth and development of countries endowed with commercially viable mineral reserves. Examples are Ghana, Guyana, and South Africa. However, with the growing concerns about sustainable development since the United Nations Conference on Environment and Development held in Rio de Janeiro in 1992, there has been increasing attention given to mining activities and their environmental and social impacts. Thus, around the world there is a call for sustainable mining, and countries endowed with mineral resources are encouraged, or pressured in some cases, to transform their policies to that effect. Such a strategic shift is in support of improved social, developmental and environmental performance in extractive industries. According to the Report on Mining, Minerals and Sustainable Development Project (MMSD) by the International Institute for Environment and Development (IIED, 2002a), countries expect that minerals development will be an engine of sustained economic growth. Local communities look forward to employment, infrastructure, and other benefits that counter the risks and impacts they experience and will leave them better off than when the project started; the industry's employees expect safer and healthier working conditions, a better community life, and consideration when their employment ends; local citizens and human rights campaigners demand that companies to respect and support basic rights, environmental organisations expect that

---

[8] Lecturer II, School of Earth and Environmental Sciences, University of Guyana

industry will avoid ecologically and culturally sensitive areas; investors expect higher returns, while consumers expect safe products produced in a manner that meets acceptable environmental and social standards (IIED, 2002).

Figure 6.1 Dimensions of sustainability

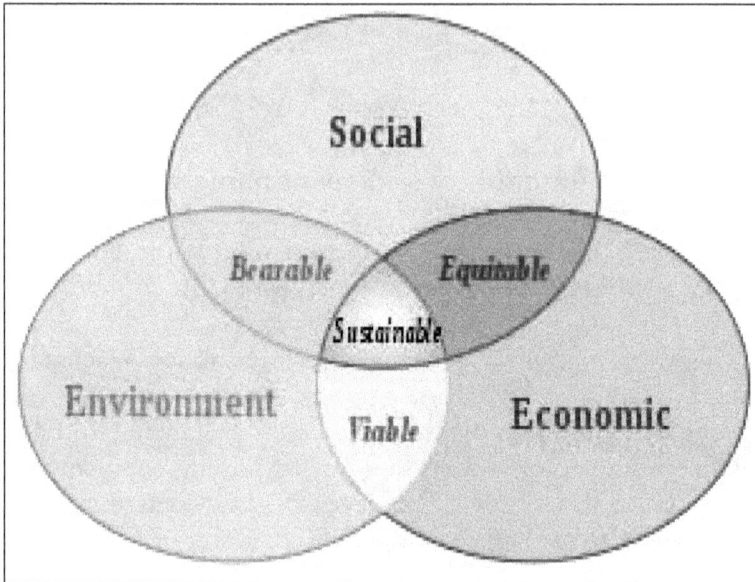

(Source: Adams, 2006)

It may be recalled that very early discourses on sustainability by the World Conservation Strategy (IUCN et al., 1980) provided a very narrow definition of the concept of sustainability by focusing primarily on the conservation of the natural environment via: maintenance of essential ecological processes and life support system; preservation of biological diversity, and; sustainable utilisation of species and ecosystems. This strategy document categorically states that 'Human beings, in their quest for economic development and enjoyment of the riches of nature, must come to terms with the reality of resource limitation and the carrying capacities of ecosystems, and must take account of the needs of future generation' (IUCN et al., 1980).

The definition of sustainability/sustainable development was improved significantly by the 1987 Brundtland Report (better known as 'Our Common Future'), which states that 'sustainable development is development that meets the needs of the present, without comprising the ability of future generations to meet their own needs, it contains two key concepts: the essentials needs of the world's poor and the idea of limitations imposed by technology and social organisation' (WCED), 1987). In summary, sustainability has environmental, economic and social dimensions and encompasses integration and interdependence of these three dimensions, as illustrated in Figure 6.1. In fact, a world in which poverty and inequity are endemic will always be prone to ecological and other crises. Therefore, sustainable development requires meeting the basic needs of all and extending the opportunity to all to satisfy their aspirations for better life, within the bounds of what is ecologically possible (WCED, 1987). Exploitation of non-renewable resources such as minerals reduces the stock of these that is available for future generations. This does not mean minerals should not be used; rather, the search for acceptable substitutes is encouraged. Technology should be used to minimise depletion and to reduce ecological footprints related to natural resource exploitation. Technology should also be socially acceptable.

Guyana: a brief overview

Guyana, with a land area of approximately 215,000 km^2, is a relatively small developing country located on the northeast coastline of the South American continent (Figure 6.2). According to the 2010 estimates by the World Bank, the population of Guyana is about 754,493 (World Bank, 2011). The foreign direct investment opportunities provided by official government policies continue to provide Guyana a comparative advantage in the area of exploiting natural resources. Over the past seven years, Guyana's economy has experienced consistent growth, with a GDP cumulative annual growth rate of 4.4 per cent for 2006-2012. Despite 2009 international economic crisis and its impact on the region and major export markets, the economy maintained an economic dynamism, growing above the region's average. In fact, Staritz et al. (2007) noted that 'for several years, Guyana enjoyed

125

one of the fastest rates of growth in the region and among low income countries, but that subsequently economic activity slowed dramatically beginning in 1998, with average growth falling from 7.1 per cent during 1991-97, to 0.6 per cent in 1998–2004, well behind the Caribbean region, and one of the lowest among highly indebted poor countries'.

Figure 6.2 Location of Guyana

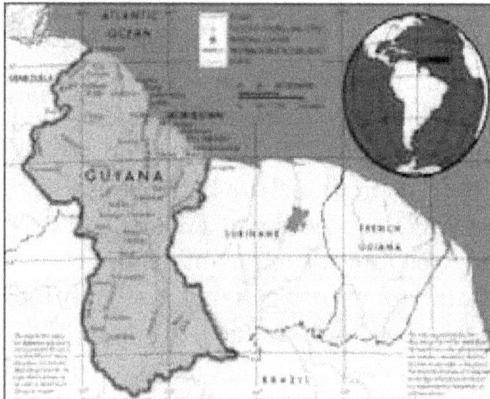

Guyana's economy grew by 3.3 per cent in 2009 (during a time of global recession) and by 2.2 per cent in 2008. Nonetheless, Guyana's external debt increased by 12 per cent to USD 933 million, representing of more than 64 per cent of GDP in 2009 (ECLAC 2012). Notably, the country's per capita GDP has been rising: in 2011 it stood at USD 2868.7. Guyana has therefore moved from a Heavily Indebted Poor Country (HIPC) status to lower middle-income country.

In Guyana, mining has maintained a strong position in the national and local economy, in terms of foreign exchange earnings, provision of livelihood opportunities, employment creation, and general social and economic development. This is comparable to Ghana, Africa's second largest gold producer, where minerals and the mining sector have played a critical role in the country's economic development process since the introduction of the World Bank-led Economic Recovery Programme (Aryee, 2001a). In fact, mining accounts for approximately 5 per cent of Ghana's

126

GDP and 41 per cent of its foreign exchange, with gold accounting for 90 per cent of total mineral exports (Aryee and Aboagye, 2008). Like Guyana, Ghana has been exporting gold for centuries.

In Guyana, mining offers significantly higher remuneration than do other natural resource sectors. It provides livelihood opportunities (mining activities, local businesses related to consumables, etc.) for households on Guyana's coast and in hinterland areas, and payments in the form of royalty, rents, taxes, and fees to the government. Mining also provides foreign exchange earnings (USD 891.9 million in 2010, with USD 346.4 million of that coming from gold alone) and the funds to develop and maintain transportation infrastructure (roads, airstrips). Table 6.1 below shows the steady increase in the contribution of gold mining to the country's GDP from 5.2 per cent in 2006 to 6.8 per cent in 2010. This is hardly surprising, given the global economic meltdown and the rise in the price of gold on the global market. To illustrate, in 2008 gold was selling for approximately USD 1000 per ounce, in contrast to the current price of approximately USD 1765.

Being capital- and labour-intensive, the mining industry employs between 15,000 and 20,000 workers, representing approximately 10 per cent of the Guyana labour force. Over the past 13 years, there has been an increase in the number of miners coming to Guyana from Brazil and entering the gold and diamond mining industries, both legally and illegally.

Table 6.1 Contribution of gold to Guyana GDP

Year	Declaration (ounces)	Export Value (f.o.b. USD million)	GDP Contribution (2006 prices)
2010	308,438	346.4	20,757 (6.8%)
2009	299,822	282.0	20,177 (6.8%)
2008	261,424	203.7	17,593 (6.1%)
2007	238,298	153.1	16,037 (5.9%)
2006	205,942	114.4	13,859 (5.2%)

Source: Guyana Bureau of Statistics National Accounts Data (On Line)

Small- and medium-scale gold mining in Guyana

The Guyana Mining Act (1989) specifically defines a medium-scale mine as one with an allowed property size of between 150 to 1,200 acres [61 to 486 ha] and a small-scale mine as one with a land claim fixed at 27.5 acres (11.1 ha). Also, small-scale mines are further defined according to the following criteria: (1) Investment of less than USD 1 million; (2) labour force of less than 100 persons, and: (3) crude ore production annual sales of less than 100,000 tonnes per year. Under the Mining Act, state lands in the mining districts can be allocated to small-, medium- or large-scale prospecting on mining, or to large reconnaissance-scale geological, geochemical or geophysical surveys (Guyana Geology and Mines Commission Mining Supplement, 2011).

Research has shown that of the two, the small-scale gold mining is more adversely affected by limited technical skills, financial resources, and new and appropriate technology (Bynoe, 2009).

In Guyana, almost all medium- and small-scale operations are placer and/or dredge mining operations (Wet recovery). Placer and dredge mining is the extraction of minerals from an alluvial deposit of sand and gravel that contains particles of gold or other valuable minerals. Placer deposits are normally located in natural watercourses or old channels high above streams. Land dredging involves the use of commercial suction hoses and mechanised sluices, which permit miners to work riverbeds and riverbanks. To flush out alluvial beds, water is pumped several hundreds of metres after which streambed materials are transfer red to a recovery system floating at the surface. The gold is then separated from the other streambed material, which is returned to the river. Miners then use mercury to further separate the gold (Ramessar, n.d). Medium- and small-scale operations recover gold almost exclusively by using mercury amalgamation. Amalgamation is inexpensive and it requires no specific skills. Metallic mercury is used to trap fine gold during mercury amalgamation. During recovery of the gold from the amalgam, mercury is discharged to tailings and/or volatilised into the atmosphere.

Recent studies seem to suggest that small-scale mining is increasing as a livelihood activity. As the Global Report for Artisanal and Small-Scale Mining (IIED, 2002b) noted, artisanal or small-scale mining activities are as important as large-scale mining activities in terms of employment opportunities they create. Additionally, most of the people involved are poor and therefore mining represents the most promising, if not, the only livelihood opportunity available to them. To date, there are approximately 10,000 artisanal and small-scale miners operating in Guyana, whereas there are approximately 300 registered small-scale mining groups in Ghana. A total of 339 active dredges in the six mining districts were registered in 2009; in 2010 this total increased by 40.4 per cent (Guyana, 2011). Moreover, in 2009 miners in small- and medium-size mines exceeded projections of 257, 503 ounces of gold by declaring the production of 305,178, which represented a 17.2 per cent increase over 2008 figures (Marks, 2010).

Small- and medium-scale gold-mining and sustainability in Guyana: critical issues

Mining makes positive contributions to Guyana's national and local economic and social development. However, the industry - and particularly small- and medium-scale gold-mining - has been blamed for numerous environmental and socio-cultural ills, including the loss of biodiversity, pollution of water, air and land, land take[9,] adverse impacts on local economies, and cultural conflicts. These issues have been brought to the fore in the wake of the growing international concerns about the sustainability of mining, as well as issues such as global climate change and sustainable forestry management. National concerns about and interests in adverse environmental and social impacts of mining grew after the infamous 1995 cyanide spill in Guyana, which plunged the country into a state of emergency. The source of the spill was the Omai Gold Mines Limited (OGLM) mining operations, owned by two principally foreign owned and registered companies: Cambior Inc. of Quebec Limited with a share of 65 per cent and Golden Star Resources Limited of Colorado with a 30 per cent share, and the Government of Guyana owns 5 per cent. The Mining Act of 1989 permitted only Guyanese citizens to undertake small- and medium-scale mining projects, while foreigners were restricted largely to large-scale mining. It should be noted that the cessation of large-scale mining became effective in

[9] Land that is being used for mining, but previously used for forestry.

2005 to facilitate a review of the environmental management systems in place for large scale gold mining.

Environmental sustainability

One of Guyana's most valued natural assets is its forests (Figure 6.3). Over the past five years the contribution of the forestry sector in Guyana has been constant at between 3 and 4 per cent of its GDP. Forest covers approximately 77.2 per cent of the country. It is estimated to contain over 5 gigatonnes (Gt) of carbon dioxide (CO_2) in above-ground biomass. With a historically low deforestation rate of approximately 0.1 to 0.3 per cent per year, Guyana is classified as being a High Forest Cover Low Deforestation Rate (HFLD) country (NORAD 2011). Further, the Low Carbon Development Strategy (LCDS, 2009/2010) argues that avoided deforestation in Guyana could deliver to the world avoided emissions of greenhouse gases equivalent to 1.5 gigatonnes of CO_2 emissions by 2020.

Figure 6.3 Guyana's forest resources

(Source: Guyana Low Carbon Development Strategy, May 2010)

It is therefore hardly surprising that Guyana has made a political commitment and promised to deploy the country's forests to tackle global warming in exchange for 'development aid' and

130

'technical assistance needed to make the change to a green economy'. Thus, Guyana has charted "an economically rational deforestation path that involves reducing forest cover by approximately 4.3 per cent (approximately 630,000 ha) per annum over the course of 25 years, leaving intact as protected areas the 10 per cent of Guyana's forests with the highest conservation value" (Government of Guyana, 2010).

Globally, combating deforestation and continuous sustainable forest management are critical mitigation strategies to limit the temperature increase on Earth below 2° Celsius (Lindhjem et al., 2009). It is believed that forest protection measures are less costly than many other measures to reduce greenhouse gas emissions (Enkvist et al., 2007). This highlights the importance of the 'Bali Action Plan' that unequivocally supported policy approaches and positive incentives relating to Reducing Emissions from Deforestation and Forest Degradation (REDD) in developing countries, and the conservation and sustainable management and enhancement of forest carbon stocks (REDD-Plus).

Guyana's REDD-Plus mechanism is linked to a wider national development policy and planning process, which is encapsulated in the Guyana Low Carbon Development Strategy 2010. This aims essentially to generate carbon credits/offsets, derived from the avoided deforestation of Guyana's forests, for commercial sale on global carbon trading markets (Laughlin, 2010). The overall goal of the Strategy is to provide 'the world with a working example of how immediate action can stimulate the creation of a low deforestation, low carbon, climate resilient economy' (Government of Guyana, 2010). To this end, there is already a Memorandum of Understanding between the governments of Guyana and Norway, in which the latter will provide Guyana USD 250,000,000 over a five-year period on condition that the country maintains the traditionally low level of annual deforestation and reduce emissions from forest degradation. The Joint Concept Note (first published 9 November 2009) outlines certain conditionalities, including Guyana's ability to deliver results as measured and independently verified against two sets of indicators: (1) enabling activities including strategic framework, continuous multi-stakeholder process, governance and the rights of indigenous peoples and other local forest communities as regards REDD-Plus, and; (2)

measurements of avoided deforestation by subtracting Guyana's observed deforestation rate against the agreed reference level, as well as the avoided greenhouse gas emissions by use of carbon density proxies10 (Government of Guyana, 2009).

Small- and medium-scale mining activities that are not self-regulated or effectively monitored for compliance pose a grave challenge to Guyana's Low Carbon Development Strategy. Annual deforestation is being monitoring, reported and verified independently and mining has been identified as one of the principal root drivers of deforestation. Sandra Grainger in a BBC News article, 'How Guyana Gold Mining Threatens its Green Future' (26 November 2011) notes that 'mining threatens what could be the greatest asset for Guyana - its pristine rainforests. It is the dilemma developing countries face - how do you balance the desire for economic growth and preserve the world's forest'. Obviously, this mirrors the complexity of sustainability. In February 2010, hundreds of gold and diamond miners in Guyana's main mining town (Bartica) protested against restrictions on tree felling proposed by the Government of Guyana as part of its USD 250 million forest-saving carbon agreement with the Government of Norway.

Water pollution is a major indirect impact of river dredging activities. Several studies (for example, the United States Army Corps of Engineers Water Resources Assessment Report in 1998 and more recently, consultations with communities have established that Amerindians' access to potable water supply is compromised due to mismanagement of tailings at several operations, and this results in high sedimentation and turbidity of water bodies. According to the report of the Guyana Environmental Capacity Development Mining Project (GGMC) (2003), laboratory results of water samples taken at Kamarang, an Amerindian and mining community at the confluence of the Kamarang and Mazaruni Rivers suggested that water used for washing, bathing and drinking was microbiologically and chemically unsatisfactory, with high coliform counts and elevated pH, lead and total iron levels. This observation was confirmed by

---

10 The aim is to convert observed deforestation rate into avoided greenhouse gas emissions and to subtract increased emissions from forest degradation, based on agreed indicators of forest degradation.

residents of Mahdia, Kamarang and Port Kaituma who complained about skin rashes, vomiting, typhoid and diarrhoea. Amerindian women in Kamarang have also complained of abdominal pains. This issue is raised by Livan (2000), who notes the siltation of drinking/potable water for communities downstream of mining operations. Given the monetary poverty of most Amerindians, the option to use bottled water is impracticable. This highlights the need to safeguard Amerindian rights and the rivers and creeks that are their source of domestic water supply. Thus, protecting creeks and rivers from pollution caused by mining and the rights of the Amerindians who depend on them are matters to be addressed by law.

A related issue is the inappropriate use of mercury. Mercury exposure in miners is either through occupational exposure to elemental mercury due to air pollution (mercury vapour), or through dietary introduction of methyl mercury, which is bound to bioaccumulation in fish (GGMC, 2003). While the mining regulations require that 'A Retort be used at all times for burning of amalgam', the reality is that this practice is hardly enforced. Stephen et al. (2004) observed that of the 31 mining operations visited along the Konawaruk River, 29 did not use retorts. Mercury also poses a threat to aquatic life and to communities that consume fish regularly.

The proliferation of malaria, due to the abundance of large, stagnant flooded pits that provide excellent breeding grounds for mosquitoes, is also a serious health impact of mining activities. The study conducted by Stephen et al. (2004) also revealed that of the 31 operations visited, 17 were using mined-out pits to trap solids (backfilling). The lack of enforcement of closure plans for open-pit mining also compromises the safety of miners and communities.

Aggregate mining generates dust and noise from the blasting and use of heavy machinery, respectively, and these both pose a health risk to nearby residents. Additionally, the dusts affect visibility and property value. In extreme cases, residents may need to relocate and be adequately compensated. However, relocation or displacement of communities can create conflicts and resentment between the miner and residents, especially if the 'new' settlements lack adequate infrastructure.

Social sustainability

There is a notable absence of tangible benefits from mining at the community level, due in part to the absence of regulations that mandate the payment of royalties (at least five per cent) to communities affected by the mining activities. A five per cent royalty, if paid into a Community Development Fund and managed responsibly, can contribute to the improvement of physical infrastructure (roads, pure water supply, energy and telecommunications), as well as the provision/upgrading of social infrastructure (health and education). In addition, young and older Amerindian males who are hired by mining operations must be paid their full wages in cash as required by law, and any kind of exploitation regarding remuneration for labour needs to be addressed urgently. Consultations held with communities showed that Amerindians are not paid by some dredge owners and that they are denied compensation for injuries. These problems arise because of the absence of clearly written agreements shaped by labour laws and of regulations regarding the involvement of Amerindians in the general labour market. For example, medical benefits must be part of the employee packages. The human capital, in terms of literacy and the negotiation power of Amerindian communities, is a constraining factor.

Further, some Amerindians communities are dispossessed of lands and resources upon which they depend for their livelihoods. In many cases, mining sites overlap with areas inhabited by Amerindians and other ethnic groups, whose livelihoods are derived from the land and other natural resources. When a mineral right is awarded, in essence it is like awarding a land right. Despite any legal distinctions, the land is removed from other productive uses for generations, and other rights cannot be exercised during mining. This increases the vulnerability of indigenous communities to food insecurity and other problems associated with lost revenue and/or livelihoods. In other instances, for example at the mining town of Mahdia, individuals' claims for small-scale mining are disregarded when large concessions are granted to mining companies or businessmen. The problem posed by land rights and mining is further compounded by the on-going disputes over titled and untitled lands, particularly, in the communities of Akawaio, Kamarang, Kaikan, Parrot Hill, Baramita, Warawatta and Kako.

There is a need to uphold by law the right of Amerindians to be involved in the decision-making process for issuing mining licences. It should be noted that the State Lands Act makes it clear that, 'Nothing shall be construed to prejudice, alter or affect any right or privilege heretofore legally possessed, exercised, or enjoyed by any Amerindian in Guyana'. However, these rights are not specifically defined. Further, any such rights must be cognisant of where the people dwell and their livelihood activities. Any agreements for mineral prospecting that the Guyana Geology and Mines Commission enters into without consultation with and the accord of Amerindians living in the area/s will definitely lead to social tensions. During the 2012 National Toshaos Conference held in Georgetown, Toshaos from the Upper Mazaruni District were quoted by newspaper journalists (Stabroek Staff, 2012) as saying, 'our waters are being polluted, destroying our fishes. The fish that we love to eat, we cannot find now. There are numerous examples where miners empowered with a permit feel that they have the authority to do as they please. Often they have little regard for the authority of Village Councils and the rules of the community.'

The fact is Amerindians are consulted in only a few cases where mineral rights are being awarded. Moreover, notification about mining concessions that have been granted is done through publication in the official Gazette and in newspapers, but the reality is that few communities and households have access to these publications. Dispossession of land leads to other issues, such as relocation/resettlement and, in specific cases, what is considered adequate compensation, and both of these need to be carefully addressed in the mining regulations.

The recent request by Amerindians for an extension of their lands has been rejected by the Guyana Gold and Diamond Miners Association, which has also threatened to take court action. Thus, a critical institutional issue is the need to create an enabling environment that recognises Amerindian rights and interests. This would include free, prior and informed consent about mining activities taking place in and around their communities, in keeping with the principle of free, prior and informed consent as elucidated by Tamang (2005) at a United Nations Workshop in 2005.

For Amerindian/community involvement in the decision-making process to be effective, it is necessary that people to be affected by a project, policy or programme are fully informed about and understand it, and they have access to adequate information about not just the project, policy or programme but also its impacts. This will be an effective way of empowering local communities to participate in the identification of concerns, potential impacts and appropriate mitigation measures (Joyce and Mac Farlane, 2002).

Governance systems for mining in Guyana

Gold mining, as a whole, can be sustainable if steps are taken to reduce the negative impacts of mining activities, and enhance its benefits by improving governance mechanisms. Some of the information presented here is taken from Bynoe and Lancaster (2010).

Organisational framework

There are several key organisations with a legal mandate to address mining issues in Guyana. These are: the Guyana Gold Board, the Guyana Geology and Mines Commission (GGMC) that was established under the GGMC Act of 1979, the Environmental Protection Agency established under the Environmental Protection Act of 1996, and the Guyana Gold and Diamond Association. Others that have an indirect interest in mining are Office of Climate Change, Guyana Forestry Commission, Ministry of Amerindian Affairs, Guyana Lands and Survey Commission, the Ministry of Health, and also NGOs, particularly the World Wildlife Fund. At a more strategic level, Guyana has established a Parliamentary Sector Committee on Natural Resources with responsibility for monitoring and oversight of line ministries and agencies involved in environmental and natural resources management. As well, as a Natural Resources and Environment Advisory Committee, chaired by the Prime Minister and comprising heads of agencies and institutions in environment and natural resources management, provides technical guidance to Cabinet on environment and natural resource policy and serves as coordinating mechanisms among sector institutions.

Duplication/overlapping of functions is particularly evident in mining, which is the leading cause of deforestation in Guyana. The overlapping of regulations governing the mining sector has significantly impeded the implementation of strategies designed to curtail deforestation. Forestry is regulated by the Guyana Forestry Commission, mining in forests by the GGMC, and agriculture within State Forests by the Guyana Lands and Surveys Commission. Miners are, however, required to give the Guyana Forest Commission six months prior notice before mining in forest concession is granted approval.

The GGMC is staffed with environmental technicians, environmental officers and mining engineers with certificates, diplomas or degrees in one of the following disciplines: Surveying, Geology/Environmental Geology, Environmental Studies, Biology/Chemistry and Mining Engineering, respectively. Four officers cited others, including Agricultural Science, Civil Engineering, while one chose not to respond. However, a study conducted by Bynoe (2009b) revealed that many officers do not have very specialised training for their specific job descriptions.

Twenty-eight male and two female GGMC officers participated in the survey. Figure 6.4 below shows the highest educational attainment of the officers: 73 per cent (22) had acquired at least a diploma. About 23 per cent of the officers surveyed chose not to respond to the question.

Figure 6.4 Highest educational attainment of GGMC officers

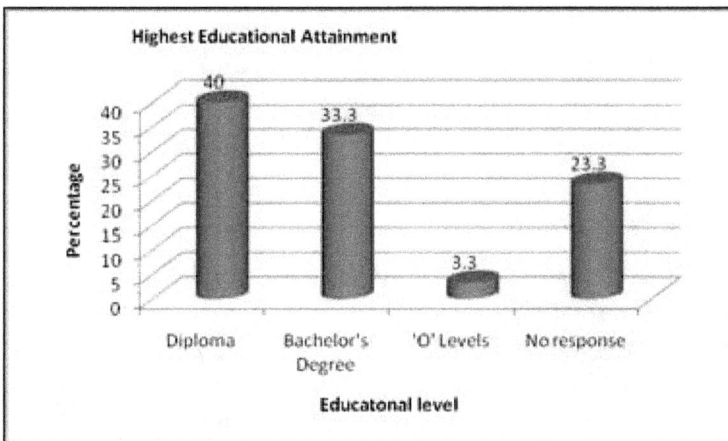

(Source: Bynoe, 2009b)

Of the 27 GGMC officers that provided responses to the question about the most challenging aspect of their job description, the most frequent answer was 'getting miners to comply with the law', followed by two others cited the same number of times, namely 'ensuring that miners adhere to regulations' and 'getting miners to consider environmental management (mine with the environment in mind)'. Respondents mentioned other challenges as well.

- getting miners to use the retort consistently
- getting miners to stop using mercury in open systems
- miners working in buffer areas language barriers
- Educating miners on environmental management issues.

One significant development is the recently established Ministry of Natural Resources and the Environment, which is tasked with the overall responsibility for forestry, mining, wildlife, environmental management, land use and institutional coordination. This initiative has been welcomed by stakeholders across Guyana, who expect this will help ensure more effective planning and decision-making in the sustainable use of the country's natural resources. Additionally, the Government of Guyana has established several strategic decision-making frameworks, including the Multi-Stakeholder Steering Group, the Guyana Parliamentary Sector Committee on Natural Resources, and the Natural Resources and Environment Advisory Committee.

Legislative framework

Guyana has a myriad legislative and policy instruments as described below.

The Guyana Constitution

According to the Guyana Constitution, Article 25: 'Every citizen has a duty to participate in activities designed to improve the environment and protect the health of the nation.' This is supported by the Constitution (Amendment) (No. 2) Act, 2003, Article 36, which states that 'the well-being of the nation depends upon preserving clean air, fertile soils, pure water and rich diversity

138

of plants, animals and ecosystems.' This provision was also enhanced by the addition of Article 149 J on the environment:

'149 J (1)   everyone has the right to an environment that is not harmful to his or her health or well-being

149 J (2)   the State shall protect the environment, for the benefit of present and future generation, through reasonable legislative and other measures designed to –

(a) prevent pollution and ecological degradation

(b) promote conservation; and

(c) secure sustainable development and use of natural resources while promoting justifiable economic and social development

149 J (3)   it shall not be an infringement of a person's rights under paragraph (1) if, by reason only of an allergic condition or other peculiarity the environment is harmful to that person's health or well-being'

Environmental Protection Act, 1996

An environmental legislative framework for Guyana was formally introduced through the Environmental Protection 1996 (Act No. 11 of 1996). This Act provides for 'the management, conservation, protection and improvement of the environment, the prevention or control of pollution, the assessment of the impact of economic development on the environment, the sustainable use of natural resources and for matters incidental thereto or connected therewith'. It has established the Environmental Protection Agency of Guyana and given the Agency the overall responsibility for oversight of environmental impact assessment, enforcement and regulation, pollution prevention or control, environmental education and public awareness, and collaboration with other agencies on environmental matters.

National Environmental Action Plan

The National Environmental Action Plan (NEAP) of 2001-2005, which follows directly the NEAP of 1994, expresses national commitment to sustainable development in the pursuit of national social and economic goals. It also provides a framework for integrating cross-sectoral environmental concerns into the wider context of Guyana's economic and social development programme (EPA Guyana, 2001-2005). This strategic planning mechanism summarises the national environment policy, and it focuses on coastal zone management, natural resources management including land resources, waste management and pollution control, and mining. Consideration is given to the role of public awareness and education in addressing environmental problems, as well as the roles and functions of relevant stakeholders including private sector and NGOs in environmental management (Guyana National Action Programme to Combat Desertification, 2006).

Land Use policy

In 2005, Guyana developed a draft Land Use Policy, although the document has not yet been finalised. When it is, the policy mechanism should provide the guiding framework for coordination among various land uses and promote optimum land use and integration. It envisages that the latter will support biodiversity conservation by optimising land use and minimising adverse impacts from competing land uses. Additionally, the Government of Guyana has established a National Land Use Committee, which comprises the Commissioner of Lands and Surveys, the Commissioner of Guyana Geology and Mines, Commissioner of Forestry, the Executive Director of Guyana's Environmental Protection Agency, and the Office of the President's Land Use Adviser. The Land Use Committee is a coordinating mechanism for managing conflicts among natural resource users. Guyana has also been benefitting from a European Union-funded programme that aims at developing land-use plans at both the national and regional levels.

Section 48 of the 2006 Amerindian Act gives responsibility to the Village Council to arrive at a decision on whether or not to grant permission to mine on village lands.

Sector legislation

The Mining Act (No. 20 of 1989) governs prospecting and mining operations in Guyana. Its chief purposes is to: prosecute defaulters; ensure standards are maintained; set standards, and; enforce compliance. Section 136 of the Mining Act makes

140

provisions for the establishment of regulations. In recognition of the sector's contribution to the country's economic development, the Government of Guyana amended its Mining Act in 1989 and the Mining Environment Regulations were promulgated by Parliament in 2005. The regulations governing environmental management for small-scale mining are similar to those for large- and medium-scale mining, except that the two latter are required to submit Environmental Management Plans. The small-scale miners are only required to submit to the GGMC for approval their clean-up plans for their site(s) in the event of a spill. The Environmental Management Plan that medium-scale miners must submit to the GGMC spells out how the miner intends to achieve environmental targets and obligations, and outlines the measures that will be taken by the miner from the planning stage of mining and then up to and including closure. The Environmental Management Plan should be for a period of 3–5 years. Miners may be required to update the Environmental Management Plan every year.

The general requirements of the Environmental Management Plans include issues relating to discharges into rivers or creeks, the use of settling ponds, the disposal of petroleum products and poisonous substances, inspection of environmentally damaged areas, responsibility of miners for environmental damage, the disposal of effluent, and tailings ponds for the waste material remaining after the gold is collected.

In addition, the general requirements provide for the Guyana Geology and Mines Commission to publish or approve a Code of Practice for Environmental Mining. Moreover, by law, miners are required to take all necessary mitigation measures to protect the environment prior to and during the course of mining in accordance with the Environmental Management Agreement that provides selected details on the mitigation measures that miners should practice during the course of mining. These are outlined below.

Mining excavation: During mining, all miners are required to refill excavations or pits within six months. Dumping of overburden in a manner that compromises water quality is prohibited. In fact, the overburden should not be placed within 20 metres of water bodies. Moreover, to secure the stability of pit faces, miners are required to put the overburden in sloping them at the angle of repose, or by using benches. This preserves the investment in excavation, guaranteeing a longer life for the working site and lessens the danger for those working inside.

Deforestation: Before any trees are removed, an inventory is needed to determine the diversity of the flora and fauna diversity within the claim and protect any important species that are identified. This should be done in consultation with the relevant authorities, including the Guyana Forestry Commission. Miners are not permitted to clear any trees that are within 20 metres from the bank of any river, creek or other waterways, to prevent or reduce soil erosion. Moreover, miners who are conducting their operations in a river or creek are not allowed to mine within 20 metres from the bank of the river or creek, providing that the river or creek has a width greater than 20 metres.

Tailings ponds: Miners are prohibited from discharging tailings directly into rivers, creeks or streams. Thus, tailings ponds must be constructed for the discharge of tailings, that is, to hold tailings while they settle. This reduces the discharge of turbid/muddy waters into rivers, creeks or streams and therefore results in clearer water being discharged. In fact, discharges from tailings ponds and mine operations should not exceed the turbidity limits set by the GGMC of 100 mg/L of total suspended solids or 50 Nephelometric Turbidity Units.

Use and handling of mercury: Miners are required to wear approved gloves and protective gear, including suitable respirators when heating or handling mercury or amalgam, to prevent exposure to mercury used only at the final stage of gold recovery. The use of approved retorts is mandatory when heating amalgam, unless the miner has the resources available to support the use of advanced technology, which must first be approved by the Commissioner of the GGMC.

Reclamation fee and environmental bond: All small-scale claim holders are required to pay a reclamation fee of 25,000 Guyana dollars (USD 125) on all valid claims disturbed or to be disturbed by mining. A reclamation fee or bond is used as a guarantee that miners will restore the land to its original condition. Medium-scale miners, however, are required to pay a precautionary deposit in the form of an Environmental Bond, as required by the Mining

(Amendment) Regulations 2005. Essentially, the Regulations state that at the time of the granting of the mining permit, the holder of the permit shall lodge, in the form of a Bank Guaranteed deposit in favour of the Commission, an Environmental Bond in such sum as may be determined by the Commission (currently, the bond is set at 100,000 Guyana dollars or USD 500). Officers have different opinions on the effectiveness of the environmental bond as a means of improving mining operations with respect to the environment (Bynoe, 2008). And as noted earlier, medium-scale miners are also required to sign an Environmental Management Agreement with the GGMC.

Contingency, emergency response and clean-up plans: Small-scale miners must submit a plan to the GGMC showing the location of all materials stored and a notification and clean-up plan for each proposed site of operation in the event of a spill.

Reclamation and closure plan: Medium-scale miners must submit a Reclamation and Closure Plan to the GGMC for approval before starting their operations. This plan should include measures that will be taken by the miner for backfilling of pits, and where applicable the sealing or capping of shafts, the stripping and stockpiling of topsoil for use in reclamation, the replacement of topsoil and vegetation of disturbed lands, and also the restoration of water courses, where appropriate.

Draft occupational safety and health regulations for mining: Draft Occupational Safety and Health Regulations for Mining are still to be approved. These regulations address issues such as competency requirements for miners, overall design of mine workings and access to workplaces, safety requirements in surface mining operations, safety requirements in underground mining operations, and emergency procedure and fire prevention control. Clearly these regulations are long been overdue and will help mitigate existing health and safety issues, highlighted earlier in this paper.

No mining licence can be issued for medium- and large-scale mining unless an environmental authorisation or permit has been issued by the Environmental Protection Agency and the GGMC is satisfied that the proposals of the application would ensure the most cost-efficient and optimal use of the mineral resources concerned.

143

The Regulations stipulate that the holder of a medium or large scale mines must keep a book, in which shall be recorded: the name of every labourer employed on the claim; the date of his arrival on the claim; the date of his departure from the claim; the cause of his departure and when possible the place to which the worker has gone; and in the case of death, the date of death the cause of death, the place of burial and the wages owed to the labourer at the time of death.

Additionally, the holder, lessee or other person in charge of the medium or large scale mines is mandated to keep a book showing, in the case of each labourer, the rate of wages, the amount earned according to contract, and the deductions, and shall furnish the labourer, on completion of his/her contract, with a properly certified account. This account shall show the amount the labourer has earned, the advances and goods received and the balances due to the labourer. Every book should be opened to the inspection of any officer, and any persons contravening this regulation shall be liable to a fine of 20,000 Guyana dollars [USD 100]. Any holder of a claim or his or her representative who refuses to comply with the Regulations regarding payment of wages shall be liable on conviction to a fine of 100,000 Guyana dollars [USD 500].

Sustainability challenges

Arguably, Guyana does have the basic institutional framework to regulate the mining sector and to promote sustainable mining practices by itinerant small-scale gold miners across the country. However, the degree of success is constrained by several factors, which can best be described as challenges and are summarised below.

Table 6. 2 Challenges to sustainability

Sustainability Challenges related to Mining	Description
Monitoring in a large area	Monitoring for enforcement and compliance by field officers (as per Monitoring, Reporting and Verification requirement of the MOU between the Governments of Norway and Guyana) is currently limited due to the relatively large number of operations and inadequate manpower, inaccessibility of some areas, plus the financial costs involved. Also involves issues such as inadequate financial and human resources and appropriate technology, which have significantly affected the ability of the government to carry out conservation attempts.
Reclamation	In the absence of credit facilities, small-scale miners must bear a huge initial capital cost to purchase equipment such as an excavator to carry out reclamation activities. More often than not, these miners fail to restore the mining area to its original condition due to the high financial cost this would incur.
Monitoring for compliance	It is difficult for field officers to monitor and regulate locate itinerant miners (similar to the term migratory 'hit and miss' miners in Accra, Ghana) who breach environmental laws.
Low Carbon Development Strategy	It is the plan of the GGMC to introduce and enforce more stringent regulations in terms of minimum land clearing and reclamation, occupational health and safety. Field officers will adopt an attitude of zero tolerance, the implication being that small-scale miners will have to invest in technology that reduces environmental degradation.
Research	The use of mercury will be banned by June 2013. Therefore, there is an urgent need for training in the use of new technologies such as centrifugal operation, shaking tables, cyanidation and floatation. Moreover, alternative sustainable livelihoods will have to be explored to ensure that some of the current miners and their families gain access to other viable economic activity.

Extension of Amerindian lands	Apart from the original title lands, Amerindian communities can apply for extension. This implies that no mining could take place in these areas, unless negotiated with the legal owners.
Accessibility to new areas	The limited infrastructure development in many interior locations (due partly to the rugged terrain and huge capital cost) could constrain miners from accessing new areas in search of gold once Amerindian lands are extended.
Capacity building	The GGMC needs to capacity of both miners and its field officers in order to raise the current levels of performance and compliance with regard to: tailings management, environmental management; management of safety health and sanitation, social relations; gold recovery systems that do not require mercury (see points under research), and; the design and application of knowledge-based systems for high mineral recovery, among others. Further, miners' adherence to the Codes of Practice and the Draft Occupational Safety and Health Regulations developed by the GGMC will require training. Already, environmental Management Systems have been developed for small- and medium-scale mining in Guyana; but successful implementation that will undoubtedly reduce many of the environmental and social impacts associated with mining depends largely on miners' understanding of and commitment to the systems.
Social issues	While Part VI, Regulations 89–99 of the Proposed New Mining Regulations (65:01) addresses the payment of royalties to the GGMC, it overlooks the principle of compensation, which may be required to recompense Amerindians and other groups or individuals for traditional rights or property rights that may have been surrendered to a mining company. Similarly, there is a notable absence of any regulation on royalties to be paid to the communities to redress, in financial terms, any negative impacts, including lost livelihoods, poor health related to air and water pollution, noise nuisance and loss of wildlife upon which Amerindians depend as a source of food.

Significantly, Chapter 22 of the National Development Strategy (NDS, 2001-2012) calls for the development of rules for compensation of Amerindian communities for the exploitation of natural resources contained on lands to which they lay claim, and outlines a policy that requires mining royalties to be paid into an Amerindian development fund. According to the National Development Strategy, 'the money should be directed back to Amerindian communities for their development, with guidelines for the use of that money. The money should not be seen as a replacement for Government allocations to the Amerindians, but as a supplement.'

Further, the payment of this royalty does not prevent the mining company or the miner from taking appropriate actions to mitigate environmental degradation, or to employ and involve the local Amerindian population in the mining enterprise.

Economic issues

Small- and medium-scale miners are required to pay a 2 per cent withholding tax on their gross revenue. They are also required to pay the import duty on mining equipment. Thus, there is a perception that there is little incentive for them to improve their technology. Further, small-scale miners experience difficulties in accessing loans from the banking sector, since these operations are considered to be high risk in nature. In Ghana, on the other hand, miners borrow money from gold-buying agents to purchase machinery to increase gold production (Hilson, 2003) This has implications for investing in environmentally friendly technologies.

Lessons from the Guyanese experience

By highlighting a number of important lessons, the Guyana case study can inform the policy-making processes of other countries, including African ones such as Ghana, Nigeria, and Botswana, in which minerals play a critical role in economic development.

First, sustainability itself is a very complex issue. In many cases, achievement of only one element of sustainability may undermine the achievement of another, due to an imbalance in policy development. Poverty cannot be the socio-economic baseline scenario for the sustainable development of any sector that has a critical role to play in national economic development. In Guyana, as in several other countries, gold mining plays a major role in addressing the tripod pillars of sustainable development, and therefore cannot be ignored. Further, the role of small- and medium-scale mining activities and their implications for sustainability in Guyana suggest that governments cannot afford to neglect this part of the mining sector. If they did, then the economic contribution of gold-mining and the livelihoods of untold numbers of citizens and households would be jeopardised; as a result major challenges may be posed to the REDD-Plus scheme in the country[11]. Therefore the search for sustainable livelihood alternatives must be seriously addressed. After all, poverty in itself is a threat to sustainability.

Second, as the global climate continues to change significantly, change that has been documented using scientific modelling projections, countries such as Guyana, with most of the forest remaining intact, will be pressured to save their forests as carbon sinks under the REDD-Plus scheme, while the opportunity costs of this remain high. Yet the mechanisms for incentivising forest protection and sustainable management remain inadequate and less than forthcoming. Arguably, where mining is a major contributor to country's GDP and foreign exchange earnings, the policy decision must be based on economic rationality and environmental sustainability. A forest-rich country should be adequately compensated to forego the opportunity cost of choosing to leave

---

[11] For example, persons may turn to the forest to pursue income generating activities such as logging or farming in forested areas.

148

the forest intact. Investment flows from other economic activities must be guaranteed. Thus, an enabling environment must be created to ensure that miners can venture into the alternative sustainable livelihood activities (mentioned in the preceding paragraph) that can be created by the 'compensation' received by governments. Sustainable mining is about assuring the integrity of ecological systems, maintaining or improving the quality of life of local people, and at the same time ensuring that operations are economically viable.

Third, the transfer of knowledge and information and training must be given prominence in the sustainable development of the mining sector. Most small-scale miners have low literacy levels and little awareness and understanding of the far-reaching social and environmental effects of indiscriminate mining practices. This problem is manifested in their perception of 'risks', and their unwillingness to implement mitigation measures. The latter is also due to the relatively high capital investment required for prospecting and actual mining.

The process that will facilitate the transition from unfavourable practices to those that are environmentally friendly requires a comprehensive training programme in two critical and inter-related areas, namely environmental management systems and environmental management.

Fourth, the development of mining and environmental legislation should always be accompanied by the provision of adequate resources to build institutional capacity for monitoring and enforcement. In Guyana, there is currently a shortage of financial, human and material resources to effectively address the sustainability concerns of mining. In reality, national priorities, including poverty alleviation, compete for the limited resources that are available.

Fifth, sustainability is also about people and requires a governance process based on social engagement with stakeholders; to ensure 'buy-in', miners need to be consulted and given the opportunity to provide feedback that needs to be considered when strategic policy decisions, such as the implementation of a Low Carbon Development Strategy, are made. On the other hand, miners need to respect and uphold the rights (human, tenure etc.) of local communities and treat them fairly and respectfully.

Sixth, clarification of tenure rights should be considered a priority for achieving sustainability in small-scale mining, especially if it is considered integral to national development. Conflicts between indigenous communities, miners and loggers create a social environment that makes it almost impossible for any of these natural resource users to work together to achieve the common goal of promoting sustainable development at the national and local levels.

Finally, the paucity of research hinders the sustainable development of small-scale mining. Research into environmentally friendly and low-cost technologies that support sustainable mining practices should be considered critical to the on-going efforts aimed at promoting sustainability in the mining sector. More importantly, research will provide the basis for the development of evidence-based policies to better govern the sector.

The way forward

It is unrealistic to expect that mining activities in Guyana - a relatively cash-strapped developing country - will cease. Therefore the best approach is to align the sector to the principles of sustainability, particularly from ecological and socio-economic perspectives, given that environment and economy are not mutually exclusive. Further, alternative sustainable livelihoods have not been fully developed or tested. To this end, a number of recommendations can be made.

- Policy-makers should integrate small- and medium-scale gold mining into the national development plan, and provide the necessary resources that build institutional capacity to help the mining sector achieve the goals of sustainability.

- Make training, with specific reference to on-going training in areas of environmental management systems and use of new technology to mitigate negative environmental impacts for field officers and miners, a key feature of capacity building. Guyana needs now, more than ever, a significant number of adequately trained professionals to streamline the mining sector along the lines of sustainability. To this end, the University of Guyana should further develop its curricula for mining engineers to include more environmental sciences and management courses. The institution should also lead research efforts at developing environmentally sound methods and equipment for small- and medium-scale mining operations. Importantly, courses should not be purely academic.

- Social engagement with miners (informed by a plan) in the initial stages of conceptualisation of a development policy based on a low carbon, resilient economy that has critical implications for forests (to which mining poses a threat) is essential for conflict management related to resource users. At the same time, communities affected by mining in Guyana must have equal and adequate representation at the various levels of decision-making regarding the location of mining activities. To this end, adequate information must be provided in a timely manner and must be regarded as that levelling tool for social engagement.

- Land tenure issues are the sources of many conflicts with regards to mining, local communities and forest degradation; therefore in a timely manner the government should allocate additional financial and human resources to address land-use issues (for example, land surveying and demarcation exercises using land information systems as part of land management). Integrated land-use planning is the only practicable response. Also, the rights of Amerindians must be safeguarded by enforcement of the existing Amerindian Act (2006).

- Miners' perception of environmental and social (including health) risks need to be significantly enhanced through public awareness and education programmes directed initially at the claim holder and the camp manager, then the miners. This must be carefully planned, given the migratory nature of the miners.

- To develop procedures that deal with the environment operationally, it is important to use appropriate environmental management systems that aim to integrate environmental responsibilities into everyday management practices through changes in organisational structure, responsibilities, procedures, processes, and resources. These systems should also include environmental and social impact assessments. This will promote continuous improvement of environmental protection on the part of miners, within a framework of their production activities. Further, in effort to improve environmental protection in small-scale mining activities, a suitable and simple environmental management system is required.

References

Adams, W.M. 2006. "The Future of Sustainability: Re-thinking environment and development in the twenty-first century." Report of the IUCN Renowned Thinkers Meeting, 29–31 January 2006. http://cmsdata.iucn.org/downloads/iucn _future_of_ sustanability.pdf [Accessed 25 April 2013]

Aryee, B. N. 2001a. Ghana's mining sector: its contribution to the national economy. Resources Policy, 27 61-75.

Aryee, B. and Aboagye, Y. 2008. Mining and sustainable development in Ghana. http://www.google.tt/search? sourceid=navclient&ie=UTF-&rlz=1T4LENP_en___ TT480&q=Mining+and+Sustainable+Development+in+Gh ana [Accessed 18 October 2012]

Bureau of Statistics .2012. National Accounts Data. Georgetown. Ministry of Finance

Bynoe, P. 2008. Report 1 on the Geology and Mines Commission officers survey as part of the environmental management training consultancy. Georgetown: Guyana.

Bynoe, P. 2009a. Avoided deforestation in Guyana: Exploring private sector financing opportunities to help translate policy into practice. Cambridge, Cambridge University Press.

Bynoe,P. 2009b. Report on Geology and Mines Commission officers survey as part of environment management training consultancy. Georgetown: Guyana Geology and Mines Commission.

Bynoe, P. and Lancaster, A. 2010. Diagnostic and analytical review of environmental governance systems in Guyana. Prepared for the Caribbean community study, prepared under the caricom and competitiveness project A32281, Georgetown Guyana.

ECLAC. 2012. Economic survey of Latin America and the Caribbean 2009-2010. Santiago, Chile: United Nations Economic Commission for Latin America and the Caribbean. Port-of-Spain. http://www.eclac.org/publicaciones/xml/4/40254/Guyana.pdf [Accessed 18 October 2012]

Enkvist, P., Naucler, T. and Rosander, J. 2007. A cost curve for greenhouse gas reduction. The McKinsey Quarterley 2007.

EPA (Guyana). National Environmental Action Plan (NEAP). 2001-2005. Georgetown: Environmental Protection Agency.

GGMC. 2003. The Guyana environmental capacity development (GENCAPD) report. Georgetown: Guyana Geology and Mines Commission.

Government of Guyana.1989. Mining Act, 1989. No. 20. Georgetown.

Government of Guyana. 1996. Environmental Protection Act, 1996. No. 11. Georgetown.

Government of Guyana.2001. National Development Strategy (NDS, 2001-2012). Georgetown: Ministry of Finance.

Government of Guyana. 2005. Mining Amendment Regulations 2005.

Government of Guyana.2009. Joint Concept Note. http://www.lcds.gov.gy/images/stories/Documents/JCN%20March%2031%2c%202011.pdf. [Accessed 18 October 2012]

Government of Guyana, 2010. Low Carbon Development Strategy. Transforming Guyana's economy while combating climate change: Georgetown: Office of the President.

Government of Guyana. 2010. Guyana`s national report on the implementation of the United Nations Convention to Combat Desertification. http://www.landofsixpeoples.com/weeklynews/sites/guyana-eng. pdf [Accessed 18 October 2012]

Government of Guyana. 2011. Geology and Mines Register.

Grainger, S.2011. How Guyana gold mining threatens it green future. http://www.bbc.co.uk/news/world-latin-america-15852970. [Accessed 25 April 2013]

Guyana National Action Plan to Combat Desertification. 2006. Prepared under the United Nations Convention to combat Desertification and Land Degradation UNCCD. Georgetown, Guyana Land and Surveys Commission.

Guyana Geology and Mines Commission. 2011. Guyana Mining Journal Supplement 2011). http://www.mining-journal.com/data/assets/supplementfileattachment/0004/276880/Guyana _scr.pdf [Accessed 25 April 2013]

Hilson, G.H., 2003. Gold Mining as Subsistence: Ghana's Small Scale Miners left behind. http://www.culturalsurvival.org/publications/cultural-survival quarterly/ghana/ gold-mining-subsistence-ghanas-small-scale-miners-lef. [Accessed 25 April 2013]

Chapter Seven

The Challenges of Petroleum Revenues: Ghana, Corruption, and Institutions

Inge Amundsen[12]

The resource curse predicament

Petroleum revenues can cause some serious corruption challenges, part of what is often referred to as the 'revenue curse'. If there are high levels of corruption and economic mismanagement, then government's take is obviously going to be reduced. The 'commissions' and 'fees' paid in bribes to a few government officials are small compared with the profits that accrue to the companies (especially when the profits are under-taxed because of corruption). Such practises hamper competition and reinforce monopolistic tendencies, both economic and political. Only a small percentage of the government revenue from the already dysfunctional fiscal system will be used for development. The larger share of it will be siphoned off and spent on consumption and preservation of power. The resource curse problem intensifies.

The economic mechanisms of the resource curse are fairly well known. One is the relative price effect, by which the increasing value of the local currency makes imports cheaper and exporting more difficult; another is the volatility of the petroleum prices, which lower investments and create uncertainty in other production sectors. Resource-cursed countries tend to suffer from over-investment in the extractive sector and under-investment in alternative production, the so-called 'Dutch Disease'. Resource-cursed countries also tend to de-industrialise.

---

[12] Senior Researcher and political scientist at the Chr. Michelsen Institute (CMI), Bergen, Norway.

In addition, resource-cursed countries tend to be characterised by increasing inequality, as the rich get richer and the poor get poorer. There is also a tendency for governments to squander income from the exploitation of extractive resources on grandiose infrastructure projects and 'white elephants'. Money is also pocketed (privatised) and exported; illicit money flows out of petroleum producing countries, sometimes in astronomic proportions.

In 2006, between USD 850 billion and 1.06 trillion left developing countries through illicit channels. These include bribery and theft by government officials, drug-trafficking, racketeering, counterfeiting, and commercial tax evasion. The figure dwarfs official aid flows of USD 103.9 billion in the same year by the 22 OECD member countries (Fontana, 2010). It is estimated that Ghana alone lost about USD 1.4 billion in 'Real Illicit Financial Flows' during the period 2000–2008 (Kar and Cartwright-Smith, 2010). This massive flow of money out of Africa is facilitated by a global financial system comprising tax havens, secrecy jurisdictions, disguised corporations, anonymous trust accounts, fake foundations, and money laundering. It drains countries of hard currency reserves, heightens inflation, reduces tax collection, hampers investment, and undermines free trade. It has its greatest impact on those at the bottom of the income scales, removing resources that could otherwise be used for poverty alleviation and economic growth (Kar and Cartwright-Smith, 2010).

The political mechanisms of the 'resource curse' are less well known. With substantial revenues from the petroleum sector, the benefits of controlling the state increase. More is available for consumption, enrichment and embezzlement. Higher government revenue enhances the 'cake' and thus the prize of controlling the state.

Furthermore, the autonomy of the state increases. It is no longer dependent on taxing the general economy. It suffices to control the petroleum sector and the revenues from it. This is the 'unearned' rents and the 'rentier' state model that economists talk about (Yates, 1996, Sachs and Warner, 2001). By controlling the state and the petroleum revenues, there is not much need for additional taxation of domestic economic activity and no need for a 'social contract' with tax-paying citizens. Those who control the state can fend off the influence of business interests, other economic interests (manufacture, agriculture), the middle class, civil society and NGOs.

These unearned rents also increase the powers of the state, as they provide the means to buy loyalty and allies, and to pay off rivals and perceived and potential opponents. The rents can be used for building 'clientelist' networks, vote buying, and to pay off the state institutions entrusted with checks and balances and oversight and control. Parliamentarians can be bought, as can electoral commissions, anti-corruption agencies, auditors and the like. In the final instance, the state elite can purchase the necessary military and security hardware and personnel needed to defend themselves against challengers. The elite controlling the state will have access to the means and necessary instruments of coercion.

The economic consequences of the resource curse are serious enough, including a relative weakening of non-petroleum sectors and the appurtenant interest groups, increasing poverty levels and social inequality, and sometimes even increasing social conflicts. The political consequences are equally disturbing, and they include cronyism, 'clientelism', authoritarian tendencies, and the undermining of the institutions that should maintain control and act as checks and balances.

Among the 'resource-cursed' countries, we find Angola, Nigeria, DRC, Sudan, Sierra Leone, Liberia, Zambia, Colombia and Afghanistan. These countries are characterised by poor economic development and a very low Human Development Index, despite substantial income from minerals and other resources. On the other hand, there are a number of countries whose natural resources seem to protect them (and even bless them). These 'resource-blessed' countries include Norway, Australia, Canada, Chile, Brazil, Malaysia and Botswana (Mehlum et al., 2006).

Economists have for some time discussed the 'resource curse' or the 'paradox of plenty', seeking explanations as to why some countries with rich endowments of resources have modest economic growth and unexpectedly little long-term economic development (Sachs and Warner, 2001, Robinson et al., 2005, Heller, 2006, Rosser, 2006, Boschini et al., 2007, Lederman and Maloney, 2007). Among the stronger economic explanations is that an increase in revenues from natural resources appreciates the exchange rate and makes other sectors less competitive, and that the volatility of commodity prices are disruptive. In particular, the negative price effect and a decline in investments 'crowd out' manufacturing and agriculture (Du Plessis and Du Plessis, 2006, Lederman and Maloney, 2007).

Political explanations and consequences

The literature also highlights political and institutional factors. According to Heller (2006), the analysis has to shift to political institutions to explain the resource curse, and according to Mehlum et al. (2006), the main factor determining whether resources will bring development success or failure is the quality of institutions. There now seems to be a convergence in economic theory that the quality of state institutions, the availability of rich resources and development outcomes are connected.

Economists are, however, mainly preoccupied with institutions that have a direct effect on economic performance, like the institutions governing the profitability of private enterprises (tax regimes, protection of property rights and contract enforcement, bureaucratic efficiency and 'business climate'). There is, however, also an entire political economy tradition of institutional analysis referred to as the 'new institutionalism', which emphasises the role of a broader set of political institutions in economic development (Powell and DiMaggio, 1991, and Hall and Taylor, 1996) .

The theory on the relationship between institutional factors (institutional quality) and the presence of abundant (mineral) resources denotes how the presence of resources and sudden substantial government income it generates negatively affects institutions. At the same time, faulty institutions also affect the economy in a negative way and even more so in the presence of high and sudden rent inflows.

Resource wealth can create forces that block the development of political institutions. First, this is because states with weak institutional capacity cannot prevent group conflicts over access to resource rents, nor can they prevent economically unproductive investments in lobbying for protection, subsidies and preferential policies. Institutions of 'poor quality' fail to protect property rights and contracts, and fail to avert entrepreneurs from rent seeking. Besides, power holders will exert political pressure to obstruct and dismantle state institutions in order to enable their extraction of rents and to protect their power positions for further accumulation.

The struggle for control of the state by political insiders, top-level bureaucrats, military officials and business interests, for instance, is particularly harmful. The presence of natural resource abundance has even led to civil wars. The war in Angola, the wars in the DRC and in Sudan are often described as conflicts over access to natural resources, with an ensuing decay of the state apparatus (Hodges, 2001, Cramer, 2003, Hodges, 2004, Ross, 2004).

'Dysfunctional democracies invite political rent appropriation; low transparency invites bureaucratic corruption; weak protection of property rights invites shady dealings, unfair takeovers and expropriation; weak protection of citizens' rights invites fraud and venal practices; weak rule of law invites crime, extortions and mafia activities; a weak state invites warlordism' (Mehlum et al., 2006).

It can be traced historically how the discovery and exploitation of rich resources has led to significant institutional weakening when the state institutions were weak in the first place. It is, however, noticeable that institutional decay and ensuing economic decline seem to follow *only* when state institutions were weak *prior* to the resources boom. A country is 'cursed' by its minerals when the discoveries and subsequent incomes are made *before* accountable and democratic state institutions have been established and consolidated; it is cursed when its institutions are not strong enough to withstand the pressure from various groups vying for access to the newly-found riches. In contrast, countries such as Norway and the United Kingdom were well-governed before oil and gas were discovered, and their institutions were thus not afflicted by the curse (Heller, 2006).

The 'resource curse' theory holds that oil dependency hinders democracy (Ross, 2001), and that more specifically, the consequences of discovering and exploiting natural resources will be negative only in authoritarian and semi-authoritarian regimes. Furthermore, such regimes in resource-rich countries are extremely difficult to democratise, because the ruling elites have both the incentives and the means to defend their privileged position.

Institutions of extraction and redistribution

There is the need to outline in detail the institutions that matter the most in the face of the resource curse. First, there is an analytically important distinction between the *institutions of extraction* and the *institutions of redistribution*. The institutions of extraction are necessary for the production and extraction of economic resources and for extracting the rents from the minerals sector, in particular. The institutions of redistribution are the institutions of power sharing (elections, checks and balances) and of revenue redistribution (infrastructure, health and education, social security and other state services).

The institutions of extraction, which enable the ruling elite to extract wealth and enrich itself, typically include institutions such as the presidency (presidential powers and the executive branch), the national petroleum companies, ministries of finance and petroleum, tax authorities and the central bank. In the absence of democratic controls, these institutions can facilitate 'primitive accumulation', unproductive investments and 'suspicious consumption'.

The *institutions of extraction* usually work relatively efficiently, even in resource-cursed countries, because they are needed. Ruling elites use these institutions for the extraction (or looting) of resource rents. Therefore, they are politically protected, sometimes above the law, and at times kept outside of the bloated and inefficient *modus operandi* of the ordinary state bureaucracy.

In Angola, for instance, the state oil company, Sonangol, as an essential tool for the empowerment and enrichment of the Angolan ruling elite 'was from the very start protected from the dominant (both predatory and centrally planned) logic of Angola's political economy. Throughout its first years, the pragmatic senior management of Sonangol accumulated technical and managerial experience, often in partnership with Western oil and consulting firms. By the early 1990s, Sonangol was the key domestic actor in the economy, an island of competence thriving in tandem with the implosion of most other Angolan state institutions. However, the growing sophistication of Sonangol has not led to the benign developmental outcomes one would expect. Instead, Sonangol has primarily been at the service of the presidency and its rentier ambitions. This highlights the extent to which a nominal 'failed state' can be successful amidst widespread human destitution, provided that (in this case, Sonangol and the means of coercion) exist to ensure the viability of incumbents' (Soares de Oliveira, 2007b).

The institutions of redistribution, which serve the purpose of sharing economic and political resources, can function rather poorly because they are largely unwanted, from the point of view of the ruling elite, which can have little interest in sharing the economic and political resources. They are only necessary to limit social unrest and power rivalries, and they are consequently manipulated politically and often side-lined.

The institutions of redistribution are primarily the institutions of power sharing; i.e., the institutions of checks and balances, but also the institutions of wealth sharing which include the institutions of economic redistribution. They are rooted in and sometimes supplement the institutions of power sharing. The main institutions of political power sharing are the parliament (legislature, national assembly) and the judiciary (high or supreme court), which curb the 'government's' and presidential and ruling elite's domination.

The parliament is important for stemming the 'resource curse' because it can (potentially) balance the powers of the president and ruling elite, reduce government rent seeking and patronage, and redistribute income. The judiciary can curtail the tendencies towards monopolies, economic crime and mafia methods. In addition, there are a number of special institutions of supervision and control, like ombudsmen, auditors and commissions. Together, these constitute the institutions of 'horizontal' accountability.

The institutions of redistribution also include the institutions of 'vertical' accountability, of popular participation, voice and control. The most important of these institutions are electoral agencies (without elections, there is no democratic accountability), well-functioning and credible political parties and opposition, and civil society organisations and media.

Elections are the most important vertical channel for stemming the 'resource curse'. Popular control is possible through elections in which citizens can elect another government, and through open political debate on economic policies and direct participation in policy-making. However, free and fair elections and genuine political alternatives are prerequisites.

Corruption in the petroleum industry

Corruption and economic mismanagement can take place all along the petroleum production value chain, corruption here being defined as 'abuse of public authority and power for private benefit' in accordance with the World Bank's rule-of-thumb definition. The costs and consequences can be severe, depending on the extent of supervision and control and of the checks and balances in the system. The more authoritarian the government, the bigger the scope for illicit elite enrichment. What follows is an outline of possible corruption problems in the petroleum sector. The list is not exhaustive, but it includes some of the problem areas that are better known and well described, in addition to some that are lesser known.

Legal framework or licences?

One of the first and most fundamental decisions a government has to make is whether to regulate petroleum production by law (a petroleum law, also called a concessionary system, which is common in countries such as Norway and the UK), or by a licence system (usually referred to as a production sharing agreement (PSA) or a production sharing contract (PSC). A PSC is typically a contract between the President of the Republic, the Minister of Energy (or Petroleum), and/or the state-owned national petroleum company and any companies chosen as onshore contractors in the petroleum industry. The contract details the specific rights and provisions these contracting partners have when taking part in a particular petroleum production field. A typical oil project could have around 100 sub-contracts uniting a large number of parties in a vertical chain from input supplier to output purchaser. Among these is one 'primary' contract between the state (or its petroleum

162

company) and the (private, foreign) company (or consortium of companies) that is superior to the other contracts.

Issues such as the concession period, taxation levels and procedures, technology transfers, environmental protection, local content, security issues, inspection and control regimes can either be determined by law, with each individual contract referring to the respective law, or it can be regulated by individual contracts that stipulate the conditions.

The latter involves a considerably higher corruption risk (Al-Kasim et al., 2008, Rosenblum and Maples, 2009). Where government officials and companies have to deal with conditions embedded within a contract, it opens it up for negotiations, renegotiations and the influence peddling that comes with it. The regulatory capacity of the state is diluted, as conflicts become subject to international arbitration rather than domestic courts, and the variations between contracts reflecting the different preferences of individual companies make government monitoring cumbersome. Furthermore, PSA contracts usually contain confidentiality clauses.

Contract transparency is critical for better addressing the resource management of the petroleum industry. With contract transparency, governments will in the long term be able to negotiate better deals, as the information asymmetry between the government and companies closes. In the shorter term, contract transparency will also help government agencies responsible for managing and enforcing contracts to collaborate. 'With contracts publicly available, government officials will have an incentive to stop negotiating bad deals, due to corruption, incompetence, or otherwise' (Rosenblum and Maples, 2009).

In addition, citizens will better understand the complex nature of extractive agreements if they are out in the open. Contract transparency will result in more stable and durable contracts, both because they are less subject to the population's suspicions and also because the incentives for governments and companies to negotiate better contracts will be increased (Rosenblum and Maples, 2009).

Therefore, host states should create robust legal regimes to govern relationships with investors instead of permitting individual contracts. Model contracts with as few variables as possible should be adopted and permissible modifications specified. This reduces transaction costs and corruption pressures by reducing the number of costly negotiations. It further reduces the technically difficult and costly regulatory oversight (Rosenblum and Maples, 2009).

Let us take Nigeria as an example. From 1985 to 1993, the military dictator General Ibrahim Babangida governed Nigeria. It was a period that proved disastrous, as President Babangida institutionalised corruption as a tool of political control. A recent report estimates that between 1970 and 2008, Nigerian leaders stole more than USD 89.5 billion from the national treasury, and that Nigeria lost more money through illegal outflows than any country in the world during that period (Kar and Cartwright-Smith, 2010).

In Nigeria, more than anywhere else, extractive political corruption occurs in the awarding of upstream licences. Under military rule, most licences were awarded on a discretionary basis by the head of state. At the height of personal power concentration under General Sani Abacha (1993 – 1998), he took control of the entire oil sector by giving the presidency full control of the national oil company and all oil trading. The president and minister in charge of petroleum resources awarded oil blocks on a discretionary basis. Fees for the blocks were negotiated behind closed doors, upfront, and were completely open to usurpation and corruption.

Although President Olusegun Obasanjo, when he was elected in 1999, set out to make Nigeria's oil block bid rounds more competitive (and held bid rounds in 2000, 2005, 2006 and 2007), these rounds also had serious shortcomings. Nigeria's *Petroleum Act* gives the minister of petroleum full authority over the allocation of licences for the exploration, prospecting and mining of oil. There are consequently no legally mandated processes or oversight mechanisms for the allocation of blocks. Besides, also in his second term as elected president, Obasanjo remained Minister of Petroleum for several years, micromanaging the petroleum sector from the presidency (Soares de Oliveira, 2007a, Amundsen, 2010).

In Nigeria, the awarding of large-scale contracts to oil service companies is also riddled with corruption. Aspiring contractors have used fake consultancy firms to channel payments to the government, manipulated their own company's financial systems to acquire extra cash, and distributed payments to representatives designated by those at the highest levels of government (Amundsen, 2010).

Furthermore, Nigeria's national oil company, the Nigerian National Petroleum Corporation (NNPC), has been used by most Nigerian presidents as a private purse. Former President Umaru Musa Yar'Adua (2007-2010) admitted that the NNPC 'has not been transparent, and it is one of the most difficult agencies of government to tackle because of vested interests of very powerful people in the country' (Nigeriafirst.org 2007). The NNPC allocates contracts which 'do not always follow advertised criteria or guarantee competitive pricing', and handles the crude sales and remittances of proceeds without, however, always remitting all revenues (Amundsen, 2010).

In Nigeria, a new Petroleum Industry Bill is currently under consideration in the National Assembly. It aims to replace all existing legislation relating to the oil and gas sector and to fundamentally revamp the institutional set-up of the industry by breaking up the powerful NNPC. It can, however, also be seen as a step in the direction of executive control of the industry itself.

'Dead meat' private oil companies

Whenever direct bribery and the embezzlement of funds from the national treasury has to some degree been restricted in an increasing number of oil producing countries, through the introduction of an improved revenue management system, another mechanism for the misappropriation of funds emerges. Increasingly, national private oil companies are set up to collaborate with international oil companies in consortia to win petroleum production contracts. These are not always genuine oil companies, however, but 'straw' companies owned by former and current government ministers, ruling party officials, state oil company directors and members of the ruling families.

According to the government's 'local content' policies, multinational companies are requested to 'invite' local national oil companies into their consortia to bid for the exploration and production of oil. These local companies can contribute very little in terms of financing, technology or other inputs, and the real ownership of some of these is in fact unknown to the operators.

165

Sometimes, they even default on their initial payments until they get their share of the profits. These are what a representative of ChevronTexaco in Angola referred to as 'dead meat companies' (in a private conversation).

According to a report on the Norwegian company StatoilHydro, in Angola it was 'in partnership with a local private oil company despite suspicions that the company's undisclosed owners may include government officials, in a country perceived to be one of the most corrupt in the world' (Global Witness, 2010). With no transparent business register in Angola and the possibility to register a company as an "anonymous limited-liability company", the ownership of private companies by political figures and their contracts with the state administration is concealed. Thus, in July 2005, Norsk Hydro was awarded a 20 per cent share of an oil licence in Angola, Block 4/05, with Sonangol (Angola's state oil company) as the operator with a 50 per cent share. The remaining 30 per cent share was split equally between two Angolan private companies, Somoil and Angola Consultancy Resources. The involvement of these two companies 'was not welcomed by Hydro', but it signed the contract, nevertheless (Global Witness, 2008).

This is also an increasing practice in Nigeria, where government officials have benefited from procedures that favour companies in which they have a financial stake. For instance, senior political leaders have reportedly manipulated tenders to benefit large logistics companies for their own private gain and officials have given preference to companies owned by their political and economic allies (Amundsen, 2010).

Corporate social responsibility

Ironically, activities and funding schemes labelled 'corporate social responsibility' can sometimes add to the corruption problems in the petroleum industry. Donations by multinational petroleum companies have an underlying profit-maximisation motive and rationale. Through 'branding' and reputation management, involvement in social projects can improve their reputation and thus increase their odds of winning contracts (Amundsen and Wiig, 2008).

These corporate objectives do not necessarily correspond with the interests of society, and there are examples of duplication of work and of projects that are unsustainable because they have no public follow-up mechanisms (schools without teachers, for instance). More importantly, it is relatively easy to manoeuvre social projects into serving the political and 'clientelist' interests of the ruling party and of the government.

In Angola, for instance, there are two basic streams of foreign private contributions from petroleum companies. The first stream (and the most important in terms of amounts) is the money paid by the commercial companies in the petroleum sector based on the signature bonus system. Signature bonuses may include a 'social bonus' component, which is either a percentage or a round sum donated for unspecified 'social projects' or broad social areas such as education and health.

The amounts for signature and social bonuses have increased considerably over the last few years, and the money arrives in tsunami-like waves following the bidding rounds. A fair estimate is that the social bonuses on oil contracts in Angola are worth at least USD 100 million per year, and steadily increasing. In 2004, Chevron paid a social bonus of USD 80 million on the extension of its licence for Block 0, in addition to a signature bonus of USD 210 million. The accounting firm KPMG, which carried out a diagnostic study of the Angolan oil sector in the early 2000s, noted before the payment of this bonus in 2004 that the management of social bonuses was opaque. The consultants were unable to find any record of which social projects benefited from such bonus payments (Global Witness, 2010).

Although the signature bonuses now figure in the state budget, the social bonuses do not. Sonangol manages these social and signature bonuses (Amundsen and Wiig, 2008). This opens up opportunities for all kinds of misuse of the funds; the companies themselves serve as the only accountability mechanism. Yet they are eager to be on good terms with the government. This enables the presidency and the ruling party to determine the physical location of projects in accordance with their political needs.

The second stream is the post-tax voluntary contributions of companies for social projects that are managed directly by the companies either through their own charity organisations (such as the Shell Foundation) or through various charitable organisations, churches, foundations and NGOs. The post-tax voluntary contributions are modest in size, but they are much more visible and actively promoted by the companies. For the operator Esso, the contribution is around USD 5 million a year through the Exxon Mobile Foundation. Chevron Texaco donates around USD 10 million per year (Amundsen and Wiig, 2008).

The problem with this is that the motivation of oil companies to provide social funds is guided by corporate objectives rather than altruism, and that these corporate objectives do not necessarily correspond with the interests of society. Besides, information about oil companies' social activities is quite opaque, and it is difficult to monitor what the companies are actually doing. It might be that petroleum companies have certain strategic advantages in project implementation as large and sometimes powerful negotiators with strong technological and political capability, but their social activities may increase the lack of political will by the government to provide services, and add to the problems of corruption and 'clientelism'.

Corruption in revenue management

The discussions above demonstrate how corruption and mismanagement can take place all along the petroleum value chain from the exploration to development and production. However, equally important in this regard is the corruption that takes place after the revenues have been collected, namely in the redistribution and spending phases. Corruption in revenue management does not differ qualitatively in petroleum-producing and non-producing countries, but it differs quantitatively. A 'petroleum boom' will intensify the corruption problem.

Political corruption involves people at the highest levels of the political system and the purpose is both to extract for private enrichment and consumption and to maintain the hold on power through favouritism and the manipulation of institutions. Political corruption can therefore be defined both with reference to the main actors involved, namely the individuals at the highest levels of the political system, and the purpose of the corrupt behaviour, which is personal enrichment and the maintenance of positions of power (Amundsen, 1999, Amundsen, 2006). In other words, political corruption may entail private and group enrichment and may occur for power preservation purposes. These two forms of political corruption are often connected. The latter process, however, is under-researched and underestimated, since much of the focus in the literature has been on accumulation.

The two processes of political corruption - extraction for private benefit and enrichment and the use of corrupt means for power preservation - are important analytical categories, especially when it comes to formulating measures to counter corruption. Importantly, the two processes are often connected. Many of the larger political corruption scandals include both aspects; large-scale bribery schemes are concluded when the extracted money is used to buy political support, and the full circle is completed when the purpose of power is wealth and the purpose of wealth is power.

Extractive political corruption

Political corruption in the form of accumulation or extraction occurs when government officials use and abuse their hold on power to extract from the private sector, from government revenues and from the economy at large. These processes of accumulation are referred to as extraction, embezzlement, rent seeking, plunder and even kleptocracy ('rule by thieves'), depending on the extent and context.

Political corruption occurs at the highest levels of the political system and can thus be distinguished from administrative or bureaucratic corruption. Bureaucratic corruption takes place at the implementation end of politics, for instance, in government services like education and health. Political corruption takes place at the formulation end of politics, where decisions on the distribution of the nation's wealth and the rules of the game are made.

Political corruption is usually also distinguished from business and private sector corruption. This is only a matter of academic classification, however, since it 'takes two to tango' and because the bribes offered by private companies, both domestic and international, are significant corruption drivers. Sometimes, corruption is indeed 'supply driven' and may benefit the 'briber' more than the 'bribed'.

169

Power preserving political corruption

The other process of political corruption, when extracted resources (and public money) are used for power preservation and power extension purposes, usually takes the form of favouritism and patronage politics. It includes 'favouritist' and politically motivated distribution of financial and material inducements, benefits and spoils. Methods include money and material favours to build both political loyalty and support. Power-holders can pay off rivals and opponents to secure election victories, buy votes and, if necessary, buy loyal decisions from electoral commissions to secure re-election. By giving preference to private companies, they acquire campaign and party funds and by paying off the governmental institutions of control, they can halt investigations and audits and gain judicial impunity.

Incumbents can use many methods to retain power, of which many are perfectly legal while others are illegal and corrupt. The corrupt use of political power for power preservation and extension may take the form of buying political support through favouritism, 'clientelism', co-optation, patronage politics and vote buying. Means include the distribution of financial and material benefits (money, gifts and rents), but also symbolic values like status and 'inclusion'. The corrupt use of political power for power preservation and extension also includes the manipulation of various oversight and control institutions, creating various 'impunity syndromes'.

Through corrupt means, power-holders can secure their hold on power by buying and manipulating the public institutions of accountability and control. Parliamentary majorities and favourable legislative decisions can be bought, as can favourable decisions and lax controls by various control agencies (ombudsmen, comptrollers, auditors, prosecutors). Even loyal decisions from electoral commissions and high courts have been bought.

It is political corruption when state resources - made available to office holders for public purposes - are used for party campaigning and electioneering in a biased, unconstitutional manner. Material support to political parties and political campaigns can also be obtained from private businesses, and will be corrupt if state resources or other advantages are offered in return.

The consequences of this form of political corruption are grave, and perhaps even worse than the consequences of extractive political corruption. Political corruption for power preservation purposes leads to bad governance in various forms, including: unaccountable and 'favouritist' political decisions; manipulated, weak and distorted institutions; lack of transparency and accountability; immunity and impunity; and elections that are not free and fair.

Ghana and its 'good governance'

According to existing statistics on corruption and governance in Ghana, the country seems to be undergoing slow but steady progress.

On Transparency International's Corruption Perceptions Index (CPI), a score of 100 stands for very 'clean'. In 2012, Ghana scored 45, up from 39 in 2011, 2009 and 2008, 37 in 2007, and 33 in 2006. This is a persistent and significant progress, and Ghana is now on par with Namibia and South Africa, and ranks much better than most countries in Africa (TI 2012).

According to the World Bank's World Governance Indicators, all indicators for Ghana also show a steady increase, at least since 2004 - 2005. Voice and accountability, political stability, government effectiveness, regulatory quality, rule of law and control of corruption have improved. Ghana is now in the 50 - 75 percentile range for all indicators (100 represents the highest level), which again puts the country on par with countries such as Botswana, South Africa and Namibia, and it ranks much higher than most African countries (WBI 2012).

According to the Ibrahim Index on African Governance 2012, Ghana scores 66.3 overall (in a range from 0 to 100), and ranks seventh in Africa (after Mauritius, Cape Verde, Botswana, Seychelles, South Africa, and Namibia). Ghana's governance indicators have steadily improved, and lie well above the African average. Rule of law, participation and human rights, and human development are the better-governed areas in the country.

According to the Freedom in the World 2012 index of Freedom House, Ghana is an electoral democracy and it is designated 'free',

171

as are all the resource-blessed countries (except for Malaysia, which is only 'partly free'). Most of the resource-cursed countries are classified as either 'not free' or 'partly free' (Freedom House 2013).

According to the Open Budget Index (OBI) of the International Budget Partnership, Ghana is a country that only provides some information to the public in its budget documents during the year. Ghana ranks 50 in 2012 (in a range from 0 to 100); it ranked 50 in 2008 and 54 in 2010 (IBP 2012). Although Ghana ranks highest in the West Africa region, the country is still in the large (middle-range) group of countries that provide some information, 'though this information is far less than what is required to obtain a clear understanding of the budget and to provide a check on the executive'.

However, while the Open Budget Survey demonstrates a dismal state of budget transparency in most oil-exporting countries (with for instance a score of 28 for Angola, 18 for DRC, and 16 for Nigeria), Ghana figures among the much better off 'mineral dependent' countries. For Ghana, the established regulatory regime of mineral extraction and exports (coal, copper, diamonds, gold, platinum, silver, tin, etc.) may well be an advantage when moving into the petroleum sector.

OBI characterises Ghana's Parliament and Supreme Audit Institutions as 'strong'. Still, IBP recommends that legislative oversight can be further strengthened by 'having a formal pre-budget policy debate prior to the tabling of the Executive's Budget Proposal', and the supreme audit institution 'can be further strengthened by having its budget determined by the legislature or judiciary (OBI, 2012).

According to the Extractive Industries Transparency Initiative, Ghana was one of the first and is now among the 17 'EITI compliant countries' in the world (i.e., found to be consistent with the EITI implementation criteria, a global standard for transparency in the oil, gas, and mining sectors). 'The country produces EITI Reports that disclose revenues from extraction of its natural resources. Companies disclose what they have paid in taxes and other payments and the government discloses what it has received. These two sets of figures are compared and reconciled' (EITI 2013).

According to the Revenue Watch Institute (RWI), 'Ghanaian authorities are making progress in improving expenditure transparency, and the country has introduced targeted legislation in recent years designed to ensure accountability, transparency and efficiency in public resource management. A key challenge for the Ghanaian government is to carry forward the transparency gains made through the EITI process for minerals amid the euphoria surrounding the Jubilee Field discovery' (RWI, 2013).

Furthermore, the secrecy surrounding mining and oil contracts is an issue in Ghana. According to RWI, there is no clear legal requirement for petroleum or mining contracts to be published, and the Ghana National Petroleum Corporation does not provide any information on contracts it enters into on behalf of the state (RWI, 2013).

In addition, individuals involved in the negotiation of Ghana's oil contracts reported that the government was concerned about companies' reactions if it committed to contract transparency (Rosenblum and Maples, 2009). Another challenge to contract transparency is the fact that the previous government headed by President John Kufour set up a separate and parallel inter-ministerial committee for oil, which reported directly to the president's office and was not related to (or accountable to) the EITI management committee. Thus, the current contracts for Tullow Oil, US Kosmos Energy and Anadarko were awarded through direct negotiation instead of an open competitive bidding process.

There is also a strong call for Ghana to enact a Freedom of Information Law and affirm the public's right to information as a critical means to bolster and promote transparency. Continued public and media discourse is taking place on this issue, and the government has expressed its intention to initiate a Freedom of Information bill, but the Parliament of Ghana adjourned in late 2012 without fulfilling the promise of the ruling party to pass a right to information law.

Conclusion

Institution building

The discussions demonstrate that there are numerous mechanisms by which power-holders and government insiders can extract from the petroleum sector. They can take bribes directly in the commissioning and contracting phases, especially when negotiating and renegotiating PSA arrangements and they can take 'signature bonuses' and 'facilitation money' up-front. Then, they can siphon money off from the national oil company, which is being used as the private purse of government officials, and they can use fake private oil companies and sub-contractors to 'free ride'.

Further, power-holders and government insiders can use the petroleum sector in different ways to preserve and enhance their positions of political power. Essentially, they can spend the 'rents' on power preservation. More specifically, they can also request donations and 'favours' from companies to acquire campaign and party funds and ensure that oil companies' CSR projects and infrastructures benefit their political allies.

To restrict these practices and thus reduce the possible impact of the 'resource curse', long-term efforts that have to be made on all fronts simultaneously have to be implemented in both the economic and political spheres. Some priorities stand out, however. In the economic realm, it is a question of reducing inequalities by supporting pro-poor policy change. It is also a question of reducing the petroleum industry's 'crowding out' effect on other economic sectors, primarily agriculture and manufacturing, by improving the business climate, by generating new economic activities and through economic diversification. This can potentially lead to the development of a middle class in the long term, which historically has proven to be the best guarantee for liberal politics.

In the political realm, it is a question of strengthening the institutions of checks and balances, accountability and control. The political response to the resource curse is the reduction of political 'monopolism' and the institutionalisation of efficient control mechanisms.

The solution to such problems lies, in particular, in the institutionalisation of public control mechanisms and in the 'ring-fencing' of informal practices. It is a question of the ability of Ghana's public as well as private institutions to control and withstand the pressures for extraction from 'privatisation' and usurpation of oil wealth and public money and practices of favouritism such as clientelism, patronage, and cronyism. This should take place at a broad front and include the horizontal institutions of accountability such as separation of powers, legislature and judiciary, and special institutions of restraint and control. It should also involve vertical institutions of accountability including political parties, elections, media, civil society and public participation.

According to available statistics, such as the World Governance Indicators, the overall picture is positive for Ghana, with significant improvements achieved on most of these indicators since 1996, and a ranking of Ghana on par with resource-rich and resource- blessed developing countries such as Chile, Brazil, Malaysia, and Botswana. This puts Ghana well above the rankings for resource-cursed countries such as Angola, Nigeria, DRC, Sudan, Zambia, Tajikistan, and Colombia. This picture is confirmed by the Ibrahim Index of African Governance, in which Ghana ranks much better than Angola and Nigeria on all governance indicators. Also according to the Freedom in the World index, Ghana is an electoral democracy and it is designated 'free'.

More specific data sets on areas deemed important for curbing 'resource curse' tendencies are harder to come by, but some data are available on elections and the parliament. Ghana's elections since 2000 have generally been considered to be free and fair by most observers, and the Parliamentary Powers Index ranks Ghana as a medium-range country, on par with Nigeria, weaker than Colombia, and better than the aforementioned other resource-cursed countries. Also, Ghana scores not as well as Brazil and Chile on this indicator, which suggests that parliamentary control of the executive is not sufficient in Ghana. This is also indicated by the OBI on transparency in the budget process. This indicator demonstrates that the government provides only some information in its budget documents, which is less than what is required for the public to provide a check on the executive. This makes the parliament and the Auditor General only 'moderately effective' as budget oversight bodies.

Data on the effectiveness of the judiciary systems is harder to come by, but data on the rule of law are easily available, and can serve as a proxy. The World Governance Indicators rank Ghana's rule of law relatively high, much better than all the aforementioned resource- cursed countries, on par with Brazil, but not as good as Malaysia, Botswana, or Chile. The Rule of Law Index rates Ghana as being as good as any of the other resource-blessed countries on average, better than Malaysia and almost as good as Brazil and Chile. From that we can conclude that Ghana belongs to the resource-blessed group when it comes to the rule of law, even when there are data discrepancies. The conclusion is further supported by some data suggesting that executive powers are effectively limited by the judiciary, and that Ghana has a particularly good human rights record.

The legal regime on accountability, transparency and efficiency in public resource management seems to be well developed in Ghana, and particularly important in this respect is the fact that Ghana is a compliant country of the EITI. Full disclosure of oil and gas revenues have begun, which is a particularly good sign. However, some of the special agencies relevant for management of petroleum resources have weaknesses. Ghana's anti-corruption agencies are only beginning to tackle high-level political corruption, although corruption control in general seems to be strong, and Ghana's Public Interest and Accountability Committee has only recently been established. Comparative data on the other institutional instruments established to manage Ghana's petroleum resources are hard to come by. Regarding civil society, Ghana scores high on freedom of assembly and association, and this is also guaranteed in the constitution. The same is the case with freedom of the press, where the Freedom of the Press Index 2011 classifies Ghana's press to be 'free'. However, it is of note that Ghana still needs to enact a Freedom of Information Law.

It is a main argument of this chapter that institutionalisation and democratisation are decisive factors that determine whether abundant resources will be a curse or a blessing for a developing country, and that a country will be 'cursed' only when the discovery of petroleum resources, for instance, is made before accountable and democratic state institutions are established and consolidated.

When it comes to Ghana, since 1996 the country has held four free and fair, competitive, multiparty elections, and the incumbent ruling party and president have twice stepped down peacefully as a result of the popular will as expressed in the elections. Further, the country's institutions have never been destroyed by civil war and conflict as was the case in Angola and the DRC, nor has it gone into petroleum production shortly after independence or under an authoritarian government, like Nigeria and the Sudan. Combining the above points with data on institutionalisation in Ghana, it seems fair to conclude that Ghana has reached a sufficiently high level of democratisation and institutionalisation to avoid the trappings of a resource curse, and perhaps even be blessed by its newly found petroleum resources.

Reference

Al-Kasim, F., Søreide, T. and Williams, A. 2008. Grand corruption in the regulation of oil. U4 Issue. Bergen: Chr Michelsen Institute.

Amundsen, I. 1999. Political corruption: An introduction to the issues. CMI Working Paper. Bergen: Chr. Michelsen Institute.

Amundsen, I. 2006. Political corruption. U4 Issue. Bergen: Chr. Michelsen Institute.

Amundsen, I. 2010. Good governance in Nigeria: A study in political economy and donor support. NORAD Report Discussion. Oslo: NORAD.

Amundsen, I. and Wiig, A. 2008. Social funds in Angola-Channels, amounts and impact. CMI Working Paper. Bergen: Chr. Michelsen Institute.

Boschini, A. D., Pettersson, J. and Roine, J. 2007. Resource curse or not: A question of appropriability. Scandinavian Journal of Economics, 109.

Cramer, C. 2003. Does inequality cause conflict? Journal of International Development 15, 397–412.

Du Plessis, S. and Du Plessis, S. 2006. Explanations for Zambia's economic decline. Development Southern Africa 23, 351–369.

EITI. 2013. Extractive Industries Transparency Initiative (EITI). http://eiti.org [accessed 17 April 2013].

Fontana, I. 2010. What does not get measured does not get done. The methods and limitations of measuring illicit financial flows. U4 Brief. Bergen: Chr. Michelsen Institute.

Freedom House. 2013. Freedom in the World 2013. Washington, 2013, Freedom House. http://www.freedomhouse.org /report-types/freedom-world [accessed 17 April 2013].

Global Witness. 2008. StatoilHydro's Libyan 'corruption' scandal shows need for oil industry disclosure laws. London: Global Witness.

Global Witness. 2010. Oil revenues in Angola: Much more information but not enough transparency. London: Global Witness and Open Society Initiative for Southern Africa - Angola (OSISA-Angola).

Hall, P. A. and Taylor, R. C. R. 1996. Political science and the three new institutionalisms. Political Studies 44, 936–957.

Heller, T. C. 2006. African transitions and the resource curse: An alternative perspective. Economic Affairs 26, 24–33.

Hodges, T. 2001. Angola: from Afro-Stalinism to petro-diamond capitalism. Oxford: James Currey and Bloomington: Indiana University Press.

Hodges, T. 2004. Angola: Anatomy of an oil state, Lysaker, Norway: Fridtjof Nansen Institute in association with James Currey.

IBP. 2012. Open Budget Index 2012 Country Summary Ghana Washington, DC: International Budget Partnership. http://internationalbudget.org/wp-content/uploads/ OBI2012-GhanaCS-English.pdf [accessed 17 April 2013]

Kar, D. and Cartwright-Smith, D. 2010. Illicit financial flows from Africa: Hidden resource for development. Washington, D.C: Global Financial Integrity Centre for International Policy.

Lederman, D. and Maloney, W. F. (eds.) 2007. Natural resources. Neither curse nor destiny, Stanford Stanford University Press/World Bank.

Mehlum, H., Moene, K. and Torvik, R. 2006. Cursed by resources or institutions. The World Economy 29, 1117–1131.

MIF. 2012. The Ibrahim Index of African Governance (IIAG) 2012. London, 2012, Mo Ibrahim Foundation. http://www. moibrahimfoundation.org/iiag/ [accessed 17 April 2013]

Nigeriafirst.ORG 2007. Nigeria to join UN/World Bank stolen assets recovery initiative. Online news December 19, 2007, http://www.nigeriafirst.org/article _7932.shtml

PowelL, W. W. and Dimaggio, P. J. (eds.) 1991. The new institutionalism in organisational analysis. Chicago: University of Chicago Press.

Robinson, J. A., Torvik, R. and Verdier, T. 2005. Political foundations of the resource curse. Journal of Development Economics 79, 447–468.

Rosenblum, P. and Maples, S. 2009. Contracts confidential: Ending secret deals in the extractive industries. New York: Revenue Watch Institute.

Ross, M. L. 2001. Does oil hinder democracy?. World Politics 53, 325–361.

Ross, M. L. 2004. What do we know about natural resources and civil war? Journal of Peace Research 41, 337–356.

Rosser, A. 2006. Escaping the resource curse. New Political Economy 11, 557–570.

RWI. 2013. Ghana: Transparency snapshot New York: Revenue Watch Institute. http://www .revenuewatch.org/countries /africa/ghana/transparency-snapshot [Accessed 12 April 2013]

Sachs, J. D. and Warner, A. M. 2001. The curse of natural resources. European Economic Review 45, p 827–838

Soares De Oliveira, R. 2007a. Business success, Angola-style: Postcolonial politics and the rise of Sonangol. Journal of Modern African Studies 45, 595–619.

Soares De Oliveira, R. 2007b. Oil and politics in the Gulf of Guinea. London: Hurst and Company.

TI. 2012. Corruption perceptions index (CPI) 2012. Berlin, 2012, Transparency International. http://cpi. transparency.org/ cpi2012 [accessed 17 April 2013]

WBI. 2012. World Governance Indicators (WGI) 2011. Washington, World Bank Institute. http:// info.worldbank. org/governance/wgi/index.asp [accessed 17 April 2013]

Yates, D. A. 1996. The rentier state in Africa: Oil rent dependency and neocolonialism in the Republic of Gabon. Asmara: Africa World Press Inc.

Chapter Eight

The Management of Strategic Resources: The Oil and Gas Find in Ghana

Joe Asamoah[13]

Introduction

As documented throughout this book, Sub-Saharan Africa is endowed with significant quantities of strategic resources and has been exploiting them for a very long time. Whereas there is hope that the strategic resources will assist the continent to develop its economy, mere mention of the resources often evokes apprehension, due to their abuse till now by some well-connected individuals. The pertinent question that arises is what precisely are strategic resources? Put simply, it is process for implementing a strategy for carrying out core management functions for allocating and managing resources for delivering a service (Crouch, 2010).

Next is the question as to whether strategic resources are difficult to manage. The problem does not lie with the resources per se, but with their management. Follet, cited in Stoner and Freeman (1989), posits that management is the art of using people to get things done and that managers reach organisational goals not by performing tasks themselves, but by arranging others to perform the necessary tasks. Considering the level of mismanagement that characterises the exploration, development and production of natural resources, particularly in Sub-Saharan Africa, the rhetorical question is whether we are poor managers or rather is it a question of having been 'jinxed?'

Since striking oil in commercial quantities in June 2007, and later in August 2007 and February 2008, Ghana has gone into a state of

---

[13] Managing Director of EnerWise Africa, a consultancy, research and development firm

ecstasy with very high expectations. The black gold is perceived as being the magic wand that can transform economies overnight, as a veritable panacea for all problems. There have been numerous debates and many articles have been published in Ghana that express the conflicting reactions to Ghana's oil find, ranging from apprehension to joy. This raises many questions. Can one assume that oil will bring more socio-economic development for Ghana than have the numerous minerals and other natural resources that have and continue to be exploited in commercial quantities?

Have Ghanaians seriously considered the risks of the 'paradox of plenty' or the 'resource curse'?' Are the government, research and academia, NGOs and the rest of society doing enough to address the possibility of having this socio-economic challenge in their backyard?

The success achieved in fast-tracking the development and production of oil from the Jubilee Field has been both a technological and logistical feat in itself. However, the fast pace of this oil development has also brought in a lot of challenges for the country that to be ready for the oil boom must develop legislation, craft appropriate policies, put in place regulatory instruments and institutions, and manage the heightened expectations of the Ghanaian public. There is also the need to nurture the emerging upstream oil and gas industry through a trajectory of sustainability.

It must also be said that the fast-tracking of oil production has contributed to the apparent constraints associated with the flagship Jubilee Field. The production challenges have been compounded by the continual injection of copious quantities of gas into the wells of this field. Simply put, the Jubilee Field is currently producing less oil than was projected. This chapter examines these larger issues and governance challenges associated with the advent of oil and gas extraction in Ghana.

Strategic resources

Strategic resources are of limited availability and of huge importance to an organisation or country. In some cases it may be difficult to identify those resources that create value for an organisation. The reason for this is that there is little understanding of how resources work together collectively towards value creation. It is thus necessary to move beyond the practice of

182

considering operating functions such as finance, sales, production, marketing and logistics as mere static entities in their respective operational areas. By viewing an organisation through the lens of resource creation for its stakeholders, the former is aided by the coming together of its various functional areas.

Hence, the management in the organisation is able to concentrate on the appropriate resources for value creation. There are two pertinent resources required for the proper functioning of the organisation, namely enabling and value-driving resources. Enabling resources include cash, human resources, relevant skills, technology and physical assets, while value-driving resources are customer service satisfaction, supplier satisfaction, product competitiveness, profitability, brand, employee satisfaction and operational efficiency. The ability of a country's leadership to distinguish between these two resources and understand their interrelationship assists in the creation of value over time. The leadership team takes ultimate responsibility for managing the accumulation and utilisation of those resources (Puente and Rabbino, 2003).

Management

According to Mescon et al. in Stoner and Freeman (1989), management encompasses the process of planning, organising, leading and controlling the efforts of members of an organisation and utilising all other organisational resources with a view to achieving the stated organisational goals. The word 'process' denotes a continuum as opposed to a single event. Another interesting feature of the definition is the fact that the key actionable words are in the present continuous tense. Again, the word 'all' in qualifying 'other organisations' connotes the idea of inclusivity. In a nutshell, if we take a country to represent the organisation, then the body politic may be likened to the members of the organisation. The interesting thing in this case is the fact that the word 'all' has not been used to qualify the word 'members'. This implies that not all efforts of the members of the body politic need to necessarily be controlled, which indicates some form of contradiction. A critical analysis of the definition provides a way out of this seeming paradox.

183

In managing the strategic resources of a country, the managers are continuously thinking through their actions in advance, coordinating the material and human resources, guiding and influencing people under their management to undertake relevant tasks, while ensuring that the country is on a trajectory to achieve its defined objectives. The question that immediately arises is: 'who are the managers?' The managers are in a tier, and using a bottom-up representation, range from supervisors, sectional leaders, heads of departments, general managers, chief operating officers, chief executive officers, the directors and chief directors of the relevant government departments, the ministers and the chief of staff to the head of state. It may appear to be a tall order, but who is to ensure that those in this value chain are up to the task?

Contextualising the impact of the oil and gas industry on the environment and society

Three ways in which the oil and gas industry affects society and the environment are climate change, operations on land and at sea, and positive or adverse effects on national economies. Nonetheless, traditionally the oil industry has had periods of greed and carelessness when not properly regulated can destroy habitats and damage biodiversity. Further, oil spills at sea have damaged mangrove forests, coral reefs and fisheries, both through major accidents and regular leakage from tankers, loading buoys and drilling rigs, and platforms. In addition, transport of oil also causes some ecological damage. For example, there were an estimated 16,000 spills during the construction of the Trans-Alaskan pipeline (Dudley and Stolton, 2002). Oil tanker accidents are well-known examples of ecological disasters that can have long-term impacts.

In general, the extractive industries in most developing countries have not succeeded in making significant contributions to sustainable development, nor have they adequately protected the environment. Many civil society organisations consider the industry as a major contributor to pollution, corruption and civil disturbance in a number of countries, particularly in Africa. There have been many international and national efforts and several institutions have been put in place to try to resolve to the problems associated with extractive industries. These include the UN Convention on Corruption in Extractive Industries, the EITI, the Guidelines for Multi-National Companies of the Organisation for Economic Co-operation and Development (OECD), and the World Bank Group's guidelines for financing projects. In order to properly adhere to the modus operandi of organisations trying to resolve problems within the extractive industries, governments have been asked to sign the International Conventions and to insist that companies sign and respect the EITI or a similar initiative (Asamoah, 2012).

Management frameworks for minimising environmental damage from the oil industry

The fact that the oil industry causes considerable amount of environmental damage can hardly be disputed. However, what is pertinent is putting in place measures to minimise this damage. To reduce environmental damage, the global recommendation is that plans for oil and gas exploitation and those to protect the marine environment should be developed within the context of national sustainability strategies, as recommended at the Rio (1992) and the Johannesburg (2002) World Summits on Sustainable Development. While oil and gas are finite resources, they can contribute to national sustainability within national energy/renewable energy strategies.

Strategic environmental assessment

A major component of national strategies for the oil and gas and marine sectors is the Strategic Environmental Assessment (SEA). SEAs are recommended by the World Bank Group, the European Union and many others, including the Extractive Industries Review (EIR). The EIR, which was commissioned by the World Bank Group (WBG), recommends that impact assessments preceding development should take into account various environmental and socio-economic aspects and be broad-based. They need to identify cumulative impacts of projects and socio-economic linkages to environmental issues. Among the parameters that need to be fully identified are social and health impacts and the effects the project will have on vulnerable groups. Further, the EIR recommends the following:

185

- The WBG should not finance any oil, gas, or mining project or activity that might affect current officially protected areas or critical natural habitat or areas that officials plan to designate in the future as protected.

- Any extractive industry projects financed within a known 'biological hot spot' must undergo additional alternative development studies.

- Clear 'no-go' zones for oil, gas, and mining projects should be adopted, according to the EIR, on the basis of this policy.

- Implementation of these zones can only be done by governments (Kloff and Wicks, 2004).

According to Patin in Kloff and Wicks (2004), it is noteworthy that to assist in decision-making on offshore oil development, countries such as Canada, New Zealand and Argentina use cartographic systems to show the ecological vulnerability and economic value of different areas on the continental shelf. Areas with high ecological, recreational or cultural value, or areas that are critical for fisheries, such as reproduction zones, are declared 'no-go' zones for the offshore oil industry. For the UK, a SEA of its continental shelf is done to predict and evaluate the environmental implications of a policy, plan or programme. Whereas a Strategic Environmental Assessment is undertaken at a strategic level, an Environmental Impact Assessment is done for a specific development or activity. The SEA is designed to look at the individual impacts and cumulative impacts on both the environmental and socio-economic structures.

Before oil development is undertaken in the UK, the Department of Trade and Industry that is responsible for offshore oil development consults the complete range of stakeholders to identify areas of concern and to establish the best environmental practice. A key early step is an SEA scoping exercise to obtain external input and define the issues and concerns that the SEA should address. These are key sources of information and perceived gaps in understanding of the natural environment, as well as key information sources and perceived gaps in the uptake of the effects of the activities that would result from oil and gas licensing.

Environmental management system

It is sensible that the SEA be followed by the development of an Environmental Management System (EMS) for the project into which the Environmental Impact Assessment (EIA) would be incorporated. The standards for all the other studies and monitoring programmes are set by the EMS. The EIA (Environmental Impact Assessment or Environment and Social Impact Assessment) studies should be done together in compliance with international norms and the recommendations of the World Summit for Sustainable Development (Kloff and Wicks, 2004).

Environmental regulation of maritime oil transport

Almost all aspects of maritime traffic are covered by international conventions. This sector is highly internationalised as the ships are often registered in flag states and the ship-owner and crew members may comprise several different nationalities. Considering the fact that vessels navigate around the globe, an accident could impact on the environment anywhere. Environmental regulation of the maritime traffic on an international level is therefore highly appropriate. International conventions are obligatory on national governments, which are obliged to implement the internationally established rules and regulations through their own national legislation. Some countries have, in addition to international legislation, written extra stringent regulations for ships that trade in their Exclusive Economic Zone, which is the 200 nautical mile zone as defined by the United Nations Convention on Law of the Sea. For example, the USA and countries of the European Union will no longer accept any single-hulled oil tankers in their ports and do not permit such oil tankers to load oil from their offshore facilities. They allowed ultra and very large single-hulled oil tankers to navigate until 2007. However, smaller oil tankers will be allowed to navigate up to 2015.

Competition for resources in Africa

Africa has been dubbed the 'virgin continent', because of its huge endowment of natural resources, some of which are yet to be exploited. In certain areas in Africa where highly strategic minerals and natural resources are located, there are constant sources of tension in the form of unending civil wars. Again, in a few cases, there is the need for equilibrium of forces to neutralise opposing interests. Arms and ammunition are displayed with reckless abandon with the aim of fuelling the tensions so as to perpetuate the pillaging spree or control of the largesse of natural resource wealth. Over the last few decades, there has been renewed interest in Africa by the West and the new superpower, China, which is increasingly becoming ubiquitous.

The question often asked is whether this renewed interest is economically driven or a classic case of re-colonisation. China considers Africa the future engine of global growth. Nonetheless, the perception is widespread that China's return to Africa is characterised by a manipulation of weak African countries with a view to controlling access to their resources, including the flooding of African markets with relatively cheap goods from the Chinese mainland. Beijing has the capability to make and implement decisions much faster that do international financial institutions and Western countries. For example, whereas it takes the World Bank about five years to conceptualise a road or railway, it takes China just six months. The speed of China's service delivery on the African continent is forcing development finance institutions in the West to speed up their processes, reduce red tape and bottlenecks, and the implementation of policies (Freemantle, 2008).

Despite its many problems, Africa is a land of promise and opportunity because of its immense natural resource endowment. It is especially for this reason that India, China, the European Union and the United States have been forming various partnerships with African countries that offer mutual rewards. China has been signing back-to-back deals with African countries in order to tap the continent's natural wealth and, in turn, foster Africa's industrialisation and development. Recently, Asian trade and investment have been increasing in Africa, forming part of the global trend towards South-South cooperation among developing nations (Nagpal, 2008).

India is following close behind China in its pursuit of oil and gas imports from resource-rich Africa in an effort to decrease its dependence on Middle Eastern nations such as Iran. While India's investment in energy in Africa is relatively small to date, it is seeking to advance its partnership with Africa and deems itself a natural market for Africa's rich hydrocarbon resources. India's partnerships with African countries have strengthened in the recent past with a boost in investments by Indian companies in nations such as Libya, Sudan, Nigeria, Egypt and Gabon. The Indo-African partnership is substantial, as Africa has the capability to play an essential role in enhancing India's oil supply security through diversification of its crude oil import sources. More importantly, Africa has 10 per cent of the world's entire oil and gas reserves, and its hydrocarbon exploration potential remains relatively unexploited. While India and China have awakened to these realities and are investing in nearly all sectors in Africa, US presence has mostly been restricted to the energy sector. Investment experts indicate that foreign direct investment flowing into Africa has more than doubled since 1998, but few US companies have invested in the region except for those in the oil and mining sectors (Alexander's Oil & Gas Connections, 2008).

The 'resource curse'

Considering the fact that a significant proportion of the resource exploration, appraisal and production in Sub-Saharan Africa have been characterised as invoking the 'resource curse', it is necessary to look at what exactly that term connotes. According to Gylfason et al. (1999), the 'resource curse' is a scenario whereby some countries and regions with an abundance of natural resources, particularly point source non-renewable resources such as minerals and fuels, tend to show less economic growth, inhibiting investment in human capital and inferior development outcomes than do countries that are less endowed with natural resources. Are these 'resource curses' generally associated with the exploitation and production of natural resources, particularly oil and gas, or is this just a fantasy of the imagination? For an informed position, it is necessary to critically diagnose the various curse claims from the standpoint of their original theoretical framework, or in the context of their current variants with a view to basing a judgement on appropriate empirical evidence (Clarke, 2010). There is a hypothesis that the resource curse occurs for different reasons, including:

- a reduction in the competitiveness of other economic sectors (caused by appreciation of the real exchange rate, as resource revenues enter an economy);

- volatility of revenues from the natural resource sector due to exposure to global commodity market swings;

- government mismanagement of resources, and;

- weak, ineffectual, unstable or corrupt institutions (possibly due to the easily diverted actual or anticipated revenue stream from extractive activities).

According to Adam (2008), some of the symptoms of the resource curse are challenges to the security of democracy, the nexus of oil abundance with violent conflicts, environmental degradation, the institutionalisation of authoritarian rule, fiscal indiscipline, and collateralisation of future oil revenues and corruption. Ghana can be considered fairly democratic given that it has successfully conducted relatively free, fair and transparent elections since 1992. A notable endorsement of Ghana's democratic credentials was President Barack Obama's decision to deliver his historic speech on Africa's institutional and democratic development in the country (Adam, 2008). It is too early for any meaningful discourse on the nexus of oil abundance and violence in Ghana, as the country has just found its first oil and no such cases has yet been reported. Ghana has, however, formed a body - the Petroleum Security and Co-ordinating Committee - to safeguard the country's oil and gas fields against terrorist attacks, sabotage and environmental pollution (Ghana Oil, 2011).

With regard to environmental degradation linked to offshore oil and gas in Ghana, there has been some mud spillage in the sea by Kosmos Energy, and that was even before the first oil was found. Subsequent to this spillage, a ministerial committee was established to investigate the incidents and to decide on appropriate punitive action. It was suggested that Kosmos Energy pay a fine. The company initially refused to pay the fine, asserting that the Minister did not have the power to enforce this under the Constitution or any other law in Ghana. Eventually, after numerous meetings between the ministerial committee and Kosmos, a final settlement in terms of the level of compensation was reached, and the company paid a fine. However, this incident

190

highlighted the weak underbelly of some of the contractual agreements the country has signed with the international oil companies within the context of national laws (Xinhua, 2011). This raises an early red flag, which calls for immediate redress. The latter may include publishing all contractual agreements and appointing an experienced team to engage with companies before finalising oil and gas contracts.

It must be pointed out that despite Ghana's awareness of the dangers associated with oil and gas exploitation, the preparedness of the country to put appropriate legislation in place on exploration and production is questionable. The bill being debated in Parliament does not address the issue of gas flaring, nor does it include sufficient measures to avert spills and mechanisms to deal with them (Adam, 2008). Additionally, Ghana has been having problems with fiscal discipline (Allen and Bougha-Hagbe, 2008).

Two unfavourable signals emanate from Ghana's legislative body - the move to expunge the proposal for a heritage fund and the passing of a bill that allows the collateralisation of oil revenues that will accrue in future. Among the unfavourable impacts of the collateralisation of oil is the potential to increase the government's appetite for borrowing, which could lead to fiscal deficits and the related fiscal sustainability challenges (Adam, 2008).

The oil and gas find in Ghana

History of oil extraction in Ghana

This is not the first time that oil has been found and discovered in Ghana. Indeed, commercial drilling for oil in Ghana took place as long ago as the latter years of the 19th century at Boka Agloe, a small village in the Jomoro district of the Western Region. 'Master Hayes', as the English oil man was known, undertook the extraction of oil. However, he did not return to the then-Gold Coast after returning to his country during World War II. According to Chief Osman, an octogenarian, the oil that was collected for Master Hayes was exported to Western Europe by sea. Oil exploitation began again in the early 1970s in Ghana, this time in Saltpond off the coast of Ghana's central region. There is currently some oil production offshore in the Saltpond and Central Basins. The oil find can be properly discussed by contextualising the formation and role of Ghana National Petroleum Corporation (GNPC), Ghana's national oil company.

Figure 8.1 Offshore oil blocks in Ghana

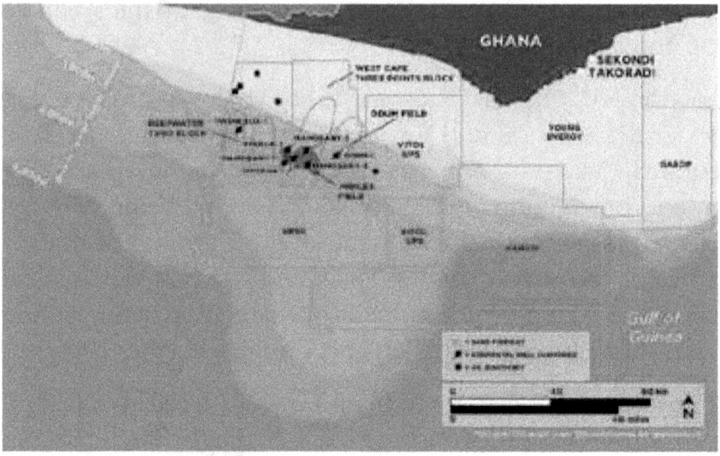

(Courtesy: kvsonghai.wordpress.com [Accessed 10 June 2012])

The GNPC was established in 1983 as a state-owned corporation under PNDC Laws 64 and 84. Its mandate is to undertake the exploration, development, production and disposal of petroleum and this is underpinned by PNDC Law 64. The legal framework that governs the contractual relationship between the State of Ghana, GNPC and the prospective investor in upstream operations is provided by PNDC Law 84. In addition, these two statutes were supplemented by the Petroleum Income Tax Law, PNDC 188 of 1987.

The enormous challenges facing the GNPC include generating international interest in Ghana's hydrocarbons, the development of young professionals (Asamoah, 2011), and natural gas transportation and processing plants (EDM and GNPC, 2011). In view of this, the corporation should, as a matter of urgency, enhance its human capital to marshal the resource flows, the cash flows and the technical details and data required to manage the oil and gas industry. Notably, the newly formed Petroleum Commission has taken over the regulatory function for the upstream oil and gas industry from the GNPC. The conclusion of a Petroleum Agreement in 2004 between the GNPC and a consortium of Kosmos Energy, Tullow Oil, Anadarko, Sabre Oil and the E. O. Group for the exploration of the West Cape Three Points Block was the genesis of modern-day oil exploration and production in Ghana. Also, the awarding of the Deep-water Tano to another consortium consisting of Tullow Oil, Kosmos Energy, Anadarko and Sabre Oil assisted in the preparation for the massive oil and gas finds in the country in June and August 2007. Since August 2007, other equally significant oil finds have been made in several wells in offshore Ghana.

Mahogany – 1 and Hyedua – 1 discovery wells

The trailblazing oil find in the Mahogany – 1 well was made on 7 June 2007 about 63 km from Half Assini and at a distance of 132 km southwest of Takoradi, an important port and oil city.

Figure 8. 2 The flag of Ghana hoisted atop an oil rig

(Courtesy: Hollis Ramblings)

On August 2007, oil in commercial quantities was again found at Hyedua, about 5.3 km southwest of Mahogany and in the Deep-water Tano oil block of Tullow Oil.

Other wells

Since August 2007, other wells, discoveries, appraisals, etc., have indicated varying commercial quantities of hydrocarbons. Among these are the Odum – 1 discovery well, the Tweneboah – 1 discovery well, the Sankofa – 1 discovery well, the Mahogany – 4 discovery wells and the Dzata discovery wells. The preparation by the consortium and GNPC to fast-track the production of oil culminated in the turning of a tap by the former President of Ghana, the late John Evans Atta Mills, on 15 December 2010 to signify Ghana's first oil extraction from the Jubilee Field. Indications are that Ghana has relatively bright prospects with respect to oil production and that only the future will reveal the extent of its endowment and production (Asamoah, 2011).

'Dutch Disease'

Oil production can be a cause for celebration, but it is also often associated with certain systemic challenges that need to be addressed to prevent it from becoming a curse. A classic case of this is the 'Dutch Disease', 'a phenomenon whereby a boom in one traded good sector squeezes profitability in other traded goods sector, both by directly bidding resources away from them and by placing upward pressure on the exchange rate' (Cordon and Neary, 1982). Dutch Disease manifests itself in the following way: deindustrialisation occurs in a nation after the discovery of natural resources, raising the value of the currency, thereby making manufactured goods less competitive compared with those of other nations. This phenomenon leads to an increase in imports and a decrease in exports.

The increase in imports has many socio-economic implications. It leads to less patronage of locally produced goods, which eventually causes the demise of local industries because of the relative cheapness of imported goods. The rise in the value of the currency makes locally produced goods more expensive than imported ones. The collapse of local industries has adverse spin-offs, including high unemployment and an increase in crime and other social vices. It is important that Ghana - a new producer of crude oil and gas - find ways to avoid the Dutch Disease' Ghana can take a cue from Norway, Trinidad & Tobago and Qatar, countries that have managed to transform their oil and gas resources into blessings.

Enabling an environment for making oil a blessing in Ghana

If Ghana is to be blessed and not cursed by its oil, it needs to implement several measures. In particular, several institutions need to be put in place, and appropriate strategies and tactics adopted. On the institutional level, an oil and gas think tank should be established without delay. This think thank needs to be staffed by professionals and technocrats from various industries and professional persuasions and should include socio-economic empiricists. The think tank should critically analyse the expected financial inflows to the country in the short, medium and long terms. It must critically project the potential impacts of these inflows, using tools such as mathematical modelling, input-output analysis and econometrics. Other measures that require urgent attention include:

- ensuring that the oil and gas revenues due to government are collected;

- regularly publishing the revenues received from oil and gas activities, and;

- active participation in the processes set up by the EITI.

Pertinent measures

Considering the prevalence of Dutch Disease in Sub-Saharan Africa, it is important to find and implement policies and measures to prevent the Disease and other symptoms of the resource curse from afflicting Ghana as it becomes an important oil producer. One solution for this hydra-headed problem may lie with the EITI, a coalition of governments, companies, civil society groups, investors and international organisations with the main aim of improving transparency and accountability in the extractives sector. Extractive industries comprise mining, oil and gas sectors. Recently, there have also been attempts to include forest resources in the extractive sector. The major component of the EITI is the publication of the revenues that extractive companies pay to governments and the revenues the governments receive from such companies. This accountability and transparency must firmly be rooted in Ghana's oil and gas and mining sectors. Among the countries that have joined EITI are Nigeria, Angola, Azerbaijan, Belgium, Canada, and United States. Other bodies which have adopted the Initiative are extractive companies, multi-lateral organisations such as the World Bank and the International Monetary Fund, NGOs including Publish What You Pay, Revenue Watch Institute, Open Society Institute and the Africa Institute for Energy Governance of Uganda (Asamoah, 2012).

Maximising returns to Government

The management of the Ghanaians' high expectations for economic development driven by the oil discovery requires a great deal attention. The government and its agencies, NGOs, research, academia and religious bodies need to work together to counter the mind-set of some Ghanaians that oil production will be a panacea for all socio-economic problems. Further, the contractual arrangements between the Government and the international oil companies need to be made public. Additionally, the following measures should be priorities that can help maximise returns to the government and potential benefits of the oil resources for the people of Ghana.

- Avoid factors that lead to political instability, violation of the human rights of people living in areas close to where oil and gas are produced.

- Prevent secrecy in contractual agreements, opaque revenue payments and avoid any increase in government budget spending as the government enters into negotiations with foreign partners.

- Painstakingly study the experiences and fallouts from the mining sector and take a holistic approach to the management of the oil and gas industry.

- Avoid the lure of an enclave economy, where employment opportunities would be available to only a few people who are connected with the top government or company officials (Freiku, 2008).

- Prioritise development projects to be funded from a dedicated oil revenue account and provide annual audits of its utilisation.

- Unequivocally implement the EITI.

- Avoid the neglect of any economic sector because of potential high cash inflows from the emerging oil and gas industry.

- Allocate special revenues to the oil- and gas-producing areas, as is the case in Nigeria for the Niger Delta region (Asamoah, 2011).

Conclusion

There is a mismatch between the poor socio-economic development of sub-Saharan Africa and its rich strategic resource endowment, particularly oil. This can be attributed partly to the scant attention that has been paid to economic challenges, such as Dutch Disease, unbridled corruption and the dearth of prudent management. Ghana has recently become an oil-producing country, and it has the advantage of being a late entrant in this sector so that it has the opportunity of learning from and avoiding the mistakes some other oil-producing African countries have made. There is, however, an urgent need for the country to establish a think tank devoted to all the issues surrounding the oil and gas industry, which can then help prevent the adverse impacts of the resource curse and instead, ensure that oil and gas become a blessing in Ghana.

References

Adam, M. A. 2008. How can Ghana escape the 'curse' of oil? .Offshore Ghana, p 31,Issue 1, February 2011

Alexander's Oil and Gas Connections. 2008. India woos Africa for resources.

Allen, R. and Bougha-Hagbe, J. 2008. 2008. Ghana aims for firmer fiscal discipline before oil flows. IMFSurveyMagazine http://www.imf.org/external/pubs/ft/survey/so/2008/CA R072908B.htm [Accessed 11 April 2013].

Asamoah, J. 2011. History of oil extraction in Ghana. Offshore Ghana, p 29. Issue 1, February 2011

Asamoah, J. 2012. Making the oil and gas find in Ghana a blessing. Accra, Ghana: Joasa Publications.

Clarke, D. 2010. Africa: Crude Continent – the struggle for Africa's oil prize. Glasgow: Bell and Bain Ltd.Cordon, W. and Neary, J. 1982. Booming sector and de-industrialisation in a small open economy. The Economic Journal 92, 825–848.

Crouch, M. 2010. Strategic resource management: Are you doing great work? http://www.nhsa.org/files/static_page_files /CCC4C2F3-1D09-3519-AD9CAD98ABB2EFF4/Modules _8_%209_and _10-Myra_Crouch.pdf [Accessed 3 May 2013]

Dudley, N. and Stolton, S. 2002. To dig or not to dig. A Discussion Paper for WWF. http://www. wwf.org.uk/ filelibrary/pdf/to_or_not_to_dig1.pdf [Accessed 11 April 2013]

EDM and GNPC. 2009. Natural gas transportation and processing project environmental and social management framework. Terms of Reference http://www.gnpcghana.com/ upload/general/tor%20for%20esmf.pdf [Accessed 11 April 2013]

Financial Terms. n.d. Definition: 'Strategic resource management'. http://www.finance-lib.com/financial-term-strategic-resource-management.html [Accessed 11 April 2013]

Freemantle, S. 2008. China in Africa: Is the continent being re-colonised? http://www.gasandoil.com/goc/news/nta8208 .htm [Accessed 8 January 2009]

Freiku, S. 2008. The consequences of oil discovery in Ghana http://allafrica/com/stories/20080416091. html [Accessed 16 April 2008]

Ghana Oil. 2011. Military committee to protect Ghana's oil and gas inaugurated http://ghanaoilonline.org/2011/01/military -committee-to-protect-ghana%E2%80%99s-oil-and-gas-inaugurated/

Gylfason, T., Herbertsson, T. and Zoega, G. 1999. A mixed blessing: Natural resources and economic growth. Macroeconomic Dynamics 3, 204–225.

Kloff, S. and Wicks, C. 2004. Environmental management of offshore oil development and maritime oil transport. http://cmsdata.iucn.org/ downloads/ offshore_oil_eng.pdf [accessed 11 April 2013].

Nagpal, D. 2008. The world at Africa's feet. http://www. gasandoil.com/goc/frame_nta_news.htm. [Accessed 20 May 2009]

Puente, L. M. and Rabbino, H. 2003. Creating value with strategic resources. http://www.iseesystems.com/community/ connector/Zine/SeptOct03/luz. Html [Accessed 12 April 2013]

Stoner, J. and Freeman, R. 1989. Management. Englewood Cliffs: Prentice-Hall International Editions.

Xinhua. 2011. Kosmos refuses to pay fine for oil spill off Ghana http://www.ghanaweb.com/GhanaHomePage/NewsArchiv e/artikel.php?ID=190803 [Accessed 12 April 2013]

Chapter Nine

Enhancing Collaborative Governance of Extractive Industries in Africa the Way Forward

Timothy Afful-Koomson

Summary of key issues

The potential for using revenues from extractive resources for broad-based development and inclusive growth in Sub-Saharan Africa is tremendous. However, the realisation of the extractive industries as engines of sustainable development has been elusive in most African countries. This has been demonstrated by discussions in the preceding chapters. The chapters have also discussed myriad challenging issues that have undermined the transformative role that extractive industries could play in sustainable development on the continent. As shown in Chapter 2, among the challenging issues are low value addition and weak linkages of the mining sector with other sectors such as manufacturing, the relatively low contribution of mining to inclusive growth despite its significant contribution to foreign exchange earnings, and the relatively low contribution to employment, income and livelihoods of adjacent communities due to its capital intensity and the enclave nature of most operations.

Other challenges include the deficient contracting systems and fiscal regimes that favour extractive companies, the mismanagement of mineral rents, weak regulatory mechanisms, low institutional and human capacity, and a lack of co-ordination between mining sector institutions. All of these have encouraged negative impacts of extractive industries, including land degradation on a massive scale, chemical and other kinds of pollution of air and water, and other health hazards and diseases. Unfortunately, because of the weak regulatory and management systems, the cost burdens of the health, ecological and social problems have been externalised by extractive industries. These issues are reiterated in Chapters 5 and 6, which also examine the environmental impacts caused by artisanal small-scale mining.

Chapters 3 discusses some aspects of the resource 'curse' and the related 'Dutch Disease' that are associated with the mining sector, while Chapters 7 and 8 examine these in the context of the petroleum sector. The symptoms of the resource 'curse' and 'Dutch Disease' include lack of diversification and over-dependence on revenue from extractive resources, low industrialisation, rising costs of living, high unemployment, disruption of economic activities and social structures of communities, and weak social infrastructure in most communities with extractive resources. Together with Chapters 4 and 9, these chapters also examine other challenging issues, such as the dysfunctional development policies for extractive resources, weak regulations and institutions, excessive rent-seeking behaviour of public officials and their corrupt 'cohorts', low financial transparency and accountability, widespread corruption, and mismanagement of revenues from extractive resources. Chapter 4 attributes most of these issues to the lack of an appropriate governance regime that could provide broad-based participation and transparent decision-making processes with outcomes of mutual benefits to all stakeholders.

These myriad issues may seemingly reflect a situation of overwhelming challenges confronting the extractive industries in Africa. While this may be true, some of the challenges are consequential and interconnected. It is important to focus on the key issues. For example, improving the use and management of revenue from extractive industries may help improve the standards of living of communities with extractive resources. It could also help to improve environmental management. A greater portion of the revenue would thus be used to take care of these problems instead of ending up in the personal bank account of a corrupt public official. As demonstrated in Chapters 1 and 4 and emphasised by the Extractive Industries Review, the African Peer Review Mechanism, and the Africa Mining Vision, having the appropriate governance regime could play an instrumental role in enhancing efficiency of the operations and management of extractive resources. It could also facilitate the transformative role of extractive industries in most African countries. Chapter 1 has examined the functionality of a collaborative governance regime for playing this role. This chapter will discuss what will be needed and what should be done to have collaborative governance regimes that may be sector-specific (mining or petroleum) and for different levels of governance, from national to local levels.

Win-win benefits and incentives for collaborative governance regime

Several factors may determine the prospects and success of a collaborative governance regime. It is important to stress from the onset that it will not be an easy process to have a collaborative governance regime. Some of the preceding chapters illustrate the pervasive antagonism, distrust and conflicts (sometimes with casualties) that have typically characterised the control and management of extractive resources and the related revenues in Africa. There are several causes, levels and dynamics of conflict that relates to extractive industries. These include disputes among public officials and also between them and politicians over the control and management of the resources and revenues. There are disputes between public officials, politicians and extractive companies over contracts, fiscal regimes, and operational, social and environmental issues. There are disputes between public officials, politicians and traditional rulers over the allocation, distribution and access to revenues from extractive resource operations. There are disputes between extractive companies and traditional rulers and their communities over resettlement issues, compensation for resettlement, social and environmental impacts of operations, development, access and ownership of infrastructure and amenities such as water and roads. There are disputes between traditional leaders and their communities over the allocation and use of revenues and funds created for community development. These conflicts have caused entrenched and outright disrespect, distrust and antagonism within, between and among all these factions. How do you get so many different factions with different interests to talk to and listen to each other for collective action?

The history of intense antagonism and bitter conflicts could hinder or facilitate a collaborative governance process (Fung, 2002,

202

Huxham and Vangen, 2004, Ansell and Gash, 2007, Johnston et al., 2010, Emerson et al., 2011). Stakeholders may have to put behind them this history of conflicts and commit to collective action to improve the extractive industries. It will be helpful to get stakeholders to look at how they are interdependent on each other for the sustainable development and management of extractive resources. For example, public officials are dependent on traditional rulers to help enforce rules and regulations. Traditional rulers are dependent on public officials for appropriations to help them 'maintain their stools' [their traditional status and power] and to develop their communities. Extractive companies, public officials and communities are mutually dependent on each other for peaceful and viable extractive operations. The fact that these stakeholders are interdependent should provide the impetus and incentive for collaborative governance (Futrell, 2003, Ansell and Gash, 2007).

It will also be useful to identify the win-win benefits available to the stakeholders within collaborative governance regime. The current adversarial regime is favouring some stakeholders and that may diminish their willingness to cooperate in a collaborative regime. However, it is important to recognise that there is a better chance of preventing events, such as deadly clashes that may destabilise extractive operations and control over resources and revenues, if stakeholders come to the negotiation and decision-making forum with the commitment to cooperate. For example, as demonstrated in Chapter 7, because some public officials are able to use the institutions of extraction and revenue distribution in an adversarial government regime to their advantage, they may not welcome the implied 'hollowed out' power that may provide other stakeholders decision-making clout. However, if politicians, public officials and authoritarian regimes had compromised for collaborative governance, some conflicts in Africa would not have escalated with such deadly consequences (Brunnschweiler and Bulte, 2009, Fjelde, 2009, Rudra and Jensen, 2011).

There are certainly mutual gains available within a collaborative governance regime and stakeholders should commit to explore these and realise such win-win benefits. For example, by working in a collaborative governance regime, public officials could expand avenues for partnership and resources to improve enforcement of and compliance with regulations, enlarge their constituencies for broader ownership of decision-making and policy outcomes, and enhance the implementation of policies and the delivery of services. Extractive companies could improve the security of their operations with collaborative governance that could reduce the risk of sabotage from some community stakeholders, and this could also help them improve their image and avoid future environmental and medical liabilities. Community stakeholders could benefit from more defined community development and collective actions for diversifying economic activities, improving employment, developing infrastructure and delivering health and social services in the community. The opportunity for realising these mutual gains could serve as the initial incentives for coming together in a collaborative governance regime. These gains cannot be attained by stakeholders acting alone and within an adversarial government regime.

Starting and managing the collaborative governance process

The processes discussed in this chapter for starting and running a collaborative governance regime are not linear, exclusive and isolated steps. They are more interrelated, cyclical, dynamic and mutually consequential. They may also vary in different sectors (such as mining and petroleum), settings and contexts. It is important to note, however, that because of its iterative nature of collaborative governance, it is essential to get the starting conditions right to provide the motivation and commitment for the process.

The need for sponsor(s) and leader(s) for the process

It is important to have a sponsor or a number of sponsors for the process (Ansell and Gash, 2007). The sponsor(s) will initiate the process and sometimes provide resources, such as staff, offices and facilities, technologies and training materials for the collaborative governance process. The sponsor may also provide guidance, evaluate, monitor and have oversight of the process to ensure cost effectiveness and to maximise impacts and outcomes from the process. Sponsor(s) could also serve as leader(s), and vice-versa, for the collaborative governance process, where applicable. It is also possible to have different institutions or individuals acting as sponsor(s) or leader(s). The leader could play several roles, including as an initiator, facilitator, convener, steward, negotiator/ arbitrator, Adviser, motivator, advocate, mediator and a catalyst. Some leadership roles, such as initiator, convener and motivator, may be critical for the process to get started. Whether at the national or local levels of governance, the leader will work to identify the stakeholders, motivate and facilitate active participation by all stakeholders, and to mobilise the stakeholders for collective action. The leader will also work with the stakeholders to set and maintain the rules and protocols for engagement, to build trust, facilitate dialogue and explore mutual gains (Ansell and Gash, 2007, Emerson et al., 2011). The leader should not only assume the traditional responsibility of being a decision-maker but should also focus on promoting, managing and safeguarding the decision-making process and ensure that the process is empowered to make decisions that are credible, convincing, legitimate and satisfactory (Chrislip and Larson, 1994, Ryan, 2001, Ansell and Gash, 2007). The diversity of the roles and the skills required for effectively executing the roles may require an institution with adequate human and financial capacity or multiple leaders.

On the character and skill set of the leader(s), it is important to stress the impartiality, credibility and competency of the leader(s). The leader should not be seen as having the tendency to prescribe rules and protocols that favour some stakeholders or advocate for decisions that are of interest to only some stakeholders of the collaborative governance process. The leader should have adequate knowledge of the technical issues and operational procedures and regulations applicable to the particular sector. For example, the leader for a collaborative governance regime on mining should be abreast with the mining codes, mining companies and stakeholders, and mining operations and/or related activities. The leader(s) should have the skills for linking issues, identifying concessions and trade-offs, for building consensus and for managing outcomes from multilateral processes. The leader(s) should have the authority and legitimacy to enforce rules and decisions that have been taken by consensus.

205

It is possible to have state, private or international agency(ies) or official(s) serve as sponsor(s) or leader(s) for the process. In African countries with extractive resources, institutions such as the United Nations, World Bank, the African Development Bank, the EITI and the New Partnership for Africa's Development (NEPAD) should consider sponsoring collaborative governance processes. These institutions have the resources, capacity and legitimacy to sponsor such processes at the national level. They can also provide the resources for collaborative governance at the local levels. However, traditional councils, religious organisations, academic institutions and extractive companies operating in a particular community could also provide sponsorship for the process. It is possible to be a sponsor without being the preferred and influential stakeholder in a collaborative governance process. There are several respectable and credible personalities within Africa that could be tapped to serve as leaders for collaborative governance of the extractive industries, at least at the national level. At local levels, religious leaders, traditional leaders and experienced professionals could make a huge difference by serving as leaders for collaborative governance of extractive industries in their communities. There should also be an opportunity for these personalities to enhance their skills and capacity if they volunteer to serve as leaders.

The institutional set-up for collaborative governance

Imposing the requirement for institutional and formal settings for collaborative governance (Ansell and Gash, 2007) may limit its application. However, as noted in Chapter 1, this requirement may be critical for improving legitimacy, transparency and accountability in extractive industries. In most countries with extractive resources in Africa, there are already informal governance arrangements with different levels of institutional set-up and interactions that exist between public agencies, extractive companies and local communities. However, because these structures and interactions are not formalised and institutionalised, most of the initiatives are mostly undertaken using ad hoc mechanisms. These informal institutional arrangements and interactions have not been effective in dealing with the legitimacy, transparency and accountability needed in the extractive industries.

The interactions between the stakeholders should be formalised and institutionalised for collaborative governance. There should be strategic and concerted initiatives to establish structure and organisation for the interactions and activities. The participation of non-state stakeholders and the roles they will play have to be formalised and recognised, just as are the formal procedures for public agencies. This will improve legitimacy and will also facilitate reallocation of decision-making clout. With formalised arrangements, non-state stakeholders can, for example, request the disclosure of financial statements, public expenditures and disbursement activities, as part of discharging their roles without 'raising eye brows' and resistance from public officials and politicians. Issues that will be discussed for institutionalisation include: representation of stakeholders; incentives that should be provided to improve broad-based participation, and; how to deal with possible asymmetry of power between stakeholders and how to enhance the capacity of stakeholders with inadequate knowledge, skills and resources for collaborative governance of extractive industries.

Representation and participation of stakeholders

Having access to the collaborative governance forum and the opportunity to participate in decision-making is very important for every stakeholder. This is the reason why the exclusion of any stakeholders in decision-making undermines the legitimacy, broader ownership and commitment to implementation and to the outcome(s) of the process. It is therefore important to identify the key stakeholders and to enhance the avenues for their participation. It is equally important to balance inclusiveness with the practicality of managing the number of stakeholders. There are several stakeholders whose interests (economic, social or political interests) are linked with extractive operations in Africa. These stakeholders include extractive companies (both large and small) directly involved in upstream and downstream activities such as exploration, production and trade in extractive resources and products. They also include companies that provide goods and services, such as equipment and legal services to extractive companies. There are public agencies, ranging from the ministries to the departments and ancillary institutions, committees and commissions. There are NGOs and institutions including traditional rulers, clans, community organisations, religious organisations and academic institutions.

However, it is not practical to manage a very large group of stakeholders. Some proactive measures are needed to balance inclusiveness with the feasibility of managing the process. One of these is to identify and include stakeholders that are the most relevant, for example, those at the national and local levels and in specific sectors or activities such as gold mining, diamond mining, and petroleum. In essence, you could have collaborative governance regimes for diamond mining and for gold mining at the national and local levels. It will also be useful to pull together stakeholders with common or related interests, mandates, goals, values, missions and demands into broader groups or associations to manage their representation for the collaborative governance regime. This should be done in a way that will not undermine the diversity of stakeholders in the collaborative governance regime.

Another possible measure is to manage the representation and participation in phases and incrementally. This means starting with a few key stakeholders and bringing in others during the process. This may be practical where there are already some formal or informal arrangements, such as committees involving, for example, EITI members, other NGOs and community stakeholders. It may also be feasible to extend the committee or group to include extractive companies and public agencies. However, this should be done carefully to ensure that those included at the beginning of the process do not become entrenched with a sense of their own prerogatives and the 'new entrants' do not feel alienated and dominated. Such measures can improve the legitimacy, cohesiveness and commitment to the collaborative governance process.

It is realistic to expect that some stakeholders may not be easily disposed to join the collaborative governance process at the beginning. This may be especially the case with stakeholders that think they could achieve their interests 'unilaterally' and independently of other stakeholders. Similarly, stakeholders that feel 'powerless' and think they may not benefit from the collaborative governance process may also abstain in the beginning. It is therefore essential to allow stakeholders to evaluate the costs and benefits of becoming part of the collaborative governance process. Sometimes key stakeholders that abstained from the process at the beginning should be provided with some incentives and resources to encourage and enable them to participate in the process. This should be done in a way that will not exacerbate power asymmetry or send wrong messages about entitlements.

Managing incentives for participation

Sometimes, incentives for stakeholders to participate in the collaborative governance process may depend on the prospect of their having the opportunity to influence decision-making. If stakeholders perceive that their involvement is just a formality and ceremonial, meant only to satisfy the requirement for representation without providing an opportunity to make any significant contribution to decision-making, they may not have the incentive to participate. Some stakeholders will also have the attitude of 'what's in for us?' They will focus on the significant outcome(s) or benefit(s) that they could get from the collaborative governance regime. Without any prospects of achieving tangible outcomes or benefits from the process, they will not have the incentive to participate. According to Ansell and Gash (2007), stakeholder expectations that the collaborative processes will yield meaningful results worth the time, energy and resources that they may be required to invest, are the best incentive to participate. The incentive to participate increases when stakeholders see a direct relationship between their participation and the tangible outcomes or benefits from the process.

There are several concrete outcomes and benefits that could be obtained from collaborative governance. For example, if transparency and accountability of revenues from extractive industries is improved, this will result in a greater percentage of the proceeds from their operations going to provide amenities that benefit communities in the operation areas, including energy supplies, water, roads, schools and hospitals. These improvements in turn can have tremendous multiplier effects for employment, household income and community development. It may be helpful to explore and communicate the tangible benefits that collaborative governance could provide. This should be done in a way that will not overly raise stakeholders' expectations for unrealistic outcomes.

Ansell and Gash (2007) also note that stakeholders will have incentives to participate in a collaborative governance regime if their perception is that the achievement of their own goals is dependent on the cooperation of other stakeholders. The incentives to participate will be low when stakeholders perceive that they can achieve their goals unilaterally or through alternative means. This may require finding and emphasising areas where stakeholders are interdependent and the mechanisms that will help stakeholders mutually enhance and reinforce the opportunities for realising common goals and outcomes. For example, one of the critical issues confronting the extractive industries is how to deal with the negative environmental impacts from their operations. Extractive companies get very bad publicity from such environmental problems. Communities where extractive industries operate tend to suffer the burden of health problems caused by air and water pollution. Public agencies, such as those involved in environmental protection, bear the costs for enforcing regulations to prevent or reduce such environmental impacts, while agencies involved with health and social welfare bear the costs for delivering health and social services required because of the presence of extractive industries. Such issues require collective consideration and action to develop the solutions that can provide benefits to all stakeholders, make the situation 'win-win' for everyone. Extractive companies will improve their image, public agencies will reduce costs and people in the extractive communities will be healthier. There may be other accrued benefits. An improved corporate image will enhance the security of an extractive company's operations and reduce incidents of sabotage. This will further reduce costs for security measures and improve productivity. The costs savings from enforcement and health services delivery could reduce government expenditure and a healthy population will improve socio-economic growth of the nation. Stakeholders should recognise that they are mutually dependent on each other and only with collective action will they realise these win-win benefits. This should serve as an incentive for stakeholders in the extractive industries to participate in collaborative governance for collective action.

Managing power asymmetry within the regime.

It is unrealistic to assume that all stakeholders will have equal voice and participate in collaborative governance regime on an equal footing. One commonly noted problem in collaborative governance is asymmetry of power (Fung, 2002, Futrell, 2003, Ansell and Gash, 2007, Johnston et al., 2010, Emerson et al., 2011). Institutions are mechanisms for exercising power and at the same time the fundamental structures for decision-making and for allocating resources, so some stakeholders will strive to ensure an even 'playing field'. This is particularly the case for stakeholders that feel they lack the capacity, influence and resources and that they could be manipulated and dominated by relatively 'powerful' stakeholders. Power imbalances within collaborative regimes should be managed appropriately.

Afful-Koomson (2012) notes that when power is concentrated in the hands of one or a few stakeholders with the clout to dominate and impose their interests and demands on the other equally legitimate stakeholders, the furtherance of concerted actions becomes very remote. Stakeholders that feel alienated, undervalued, manipulated or dominated could boycott or sabotage implementation of decisions. They could also exit the decision-making process altogether, or even resort to violence as the alternative dispute resolution mechanism. As noted in Chapter 1, there is wide array of evidence from the extractive sector where 'powerless' stakeholders have opted for armed conflict as a countervailing power because of the power asymmetry of the adversarial and top-down government decision-making system.

Enhancing the capacity of stakeholders.

Most of these 'powerless' stakeholders that have resorted to armed conflicts in countries with extractive resources tend to be less-organised, and lack the knowledge, skills, resources and capacity to engage in formal, non-violent dispute resolution and decision-making processes. It is therefore imperative to enhance their capacity for collective action within a collaborative governance regime.

Sponsor(s) of collaborative governance regimes should provide adequate resources and should commit to strategic measures to improve the knowledge, skill and capacity of 'weaker' and diffused stakeholders. Weaker stakeholders should for example, be provided with expertise to understand, analyse and interpret basic data and information on the operations of extractive industries. This is crucial for their participation in decision-making within the collaborative governance forum. There should be training initiatives to improve their knowledge and understanding on the critical issues of decision-making, including issues such as resettlement of displaced community residents, estimation of and mechanisms for payment of compensation, and management of the environmental impacts of extractive operations. As noted in Chapter 1, what is the value of participating in decision-making to improve financial transparency and accountability if some of the stakeholders in a collaborative governance regime have no knowledge and capacity to understand accounting principles, budgeting, revenue and expenditure management? The capacity of 'weak' stakeholders should also be enhanced for multilateral decision-making and dispute resolution processes. Their organisational and administrative capacities should also be strengthened.

Stakeholders should be provided with adequate human, financial and technical resources for collaborative governance. Investing in such resources is worthwhile because the governance can help ensure peace and improve security of operations, financial transparency and accountability, and environmental protection. This investment should be weighed against the high costs of armed conflicts, corruption and environmental degradation. There should be adequate financial resources to budget and to fund decision-making and implementation of critical issues. Stakeholders should be provided with the facilities and logistics, including computers, vehicles and offices to support the collaborative governance regime. According to Emerson, et al. (2011), resources could be leveraged and redistributed as shared resources in pursuit of the common goals of the collaborative governance regime. This is important because the legitimacy and efficacy of collaborative governance regimes are improved when resources are distributed fairly and differences in resource capacities are managed appropriately.

212

Setting the rules of engagement

It is important to maintain order, integrity and decorum during stakeholders' engagement within a collaborative governance regime. The decision-making process should also be transparent and legitimate. This is important for levelling the playing field and for avoiding the process being 'hijacked' by a few powerful stakeholders. This will also ensure that there are no covert or overt manipulations of the process by any stakeholder. According to Ansell & Gash (2007), setting clear ground rules and ensuring process transparency are important design features of a collaborative governance regime. They improve the legitimacy, transparency and management of the regime. They may also help to build trust among stakeholders since there are clear rules of and procedures for engagement. Rules of engagement may range from informal ones, such as ground rules, operating procedures and decision-making rules, to more formal and permanent ones, such as by-laws, rules and regulations (Ansell and Gash, 2007, Emerson et al., 2011).

Prioritising issues and articulating interests.

Once leader(s) and sponsor(s) have initiated the processes for putting the group together and rules and protocols are laid out, the focus can be expected to shift to handling substantive issues. As has been evident throughout this book, several critical issues confront extractive industries in Africa. Some might find the situation overwhelming when all these issues are viewed together. It is important to know that some of the issues are related and can thus be addressed over time, with incremental and sequential successes that are the outcomes of collaborative decision-making processes. It is also important to identify issues that should be the focus of a particular level of decision-making. For example, at the national level, the collaborative governance regime could focus on issues involving effective and transparent systems of contracting, improving local content, enhancing backward and forward linkages for comprehensive extractive resource development, and improving the fiscal system. It could also focus on developing effective expenditure and revenue management systems, eliminating legal and regulatory barriers, harmonising sector rules and activities, and improving inter-agency coordination for better enforcement of social, economic and environmental regulations. At the local level, the collaborative governance regime could focus on issues such as controlling pollution of air, soil and water from extractive operations and dealing with the delivery of social and health services to cater for victims of such pollution. It could also focus on the access, allocation and use of amenities such as water, energy and roads, and resettlement and compensation for households displaced as result of extractive operations.

It is very important to ensure that 'weaker' stakeholders are given a voice to articulate their interests and positions. This is particularly important for stakeholders that are not well organised and that have a low capacity for formal negotiations. It is crucial to separate their interests (what they want) from their positions (what they say). Sometimes, they may be saying things that are consistent with their demands and at other times there may be less consistency between the two. For example, there is a difference between community stakeholders saying they are not going to move from where extractive resources have been discovered and extractive operations are planned (position), and their request for compensation for losing their homes, lands, and income (interests).

The diversity of stakeholders in the collaborative governance regime will inevitably also involve divergent interests, positions, demands and expectations on these issues. There should be the flexibility for issue linkages. For example, linking the issues of access to water resources for extractive operations with the provision of portable water for communities and arrangements for reimbursing the medical costs of community members who become sick as a result of drinking 'polluted' water. Despite the diversity of interests and positions, there could be opportunities for aligning interests and expectations to formulate common interests on issues. This is where the facilitative role of the sponsor(s) or leader(s) will be critically needed. It is important to gain some level of consensus on which issues should be prioritised given the limited resources, time and energy available to the collaborative process.

Making decisions and developing shared understanding.

This is 'where the rubber meets the road'. There is an urgent need for joint efforts to decide the best approach(es), measure(s) and modality(ies) for dealing with issues confronting the extractive industries. This phase of the process will involve making policies, rules, or designing tools, indicators or mechanisms as part of the efforts to find solution(s) to the issues. It will also involve efforts to define, conceptualise or understand the substance of the issue or to investigate and find the root causes of the issues.

It is always very important for all stakeholders to know that they have equal opportunity to influence decisions for finding solution(s) to the issue(s) under consideration. This is the case at all levels, be it decisions made at the national level to strengthen institutions responsible for managing extractive revenues, or decisions at the local level to allocate and manage the use of water between extractive companies and communities. When some stakeholders feel that they do not have equal access to and influence in the decision-making arena, they may tend to withdraw, or sabotage the process. This will undermine the ownership, legitimacy and collective commitment for decision-making and problem solving. It may also undermine a shared understanding of the issues and decision outcomes.

Sometimes, it may be more realistic to assign stakeholders to groups according to their relative capacity, skills and resources to handle specific aspect or phase of the decision-making. For example, in dealing with resettlement issues, one group could be assigned to estimate the values for the houses, lands and household incomes that may be affected, another group may be responsible for assessing alternative settlement areas, while another group may be responsible for estimating compensations, the mechanism of payments and how to deal with vulnerable groups that originally had no houses, lands or income-generating activities. This may be both a cost-effective and a time-saving measure. Of course, the groups will have to present their findings and recommendations for all the stakeholders who will then deliberate on them as they work towards consensus building. This may involve exploring the scope for common interests, negotiating concessions and trade-offs, sourcing and making deals, harmonising interests and ideas, and facilitating shared understanding of the issues.

It is important to reiterate the need to enhance the capacity of representatives from 'weak' and 'diffused' stakeholder groups. Decision-making may require several skills and expertise, including in communication, negotiation, planning, and consensus building. Enhancing these capacity and skills will not only improve their broad-based participation in decision-making but will also make them valuable participants and improve the quality of decisions taken.

Implementing decisions and managing outcomes.

It is only through implementation of its policies and decisions that the collaborative governance regime will realise its value. And good policies and decisions only assume their meaning after their implementation and outcomes are evaluated. Without implementation, they may be wasted on the 'shelf'. Achieving the desired outcomes and impacts through implementation is very important to sustain commitment to the process. The collaborative engagement must generate some meaningful outcomes and impacts for stakeholders to justify their continued involvement to their own organisations and constituents (Emerson, et al., 2011). Implementation may involve carrying out an agreed agenda, assigning work or activities, and carrying out those activities such as cleaning polluted rivers, evacuating displaced communities, monitoring activities of artisanal small-scale miners, setting up and disbursing funds for community development, and enforcing compliance to environmental regulations.

Implementation usually occurs rapidly when stakeholders are able to achieve a working consensus on issues (Ansell and Gash, 2007). This is one of the reasons that stakeholders must own the decision-making process. Ownership to decisions taken will improve commitment to the outcomes through implementation. Implementation could also be improved if roles are identified and assigned. For example, at the local level, some stakeholders could be assigned to enforce the rules, while others could be assigned to encourage the community or enhance their capacity to comply with the regulations. Whatever the case may be, the implementation of the decisions and policies should generate some significant results. The outcomes could be small, but sequential and incremental. Though small, incremental outcomes could help deepen trust, commitment and shared understanding and thus result in a virtuous cycle of collaboration (Ansell and Gash, 2007). Trust, commitment and shared motivation are prerequisites for sustaining the collaborative governance process (Huxham and Vangen, 2004, Ansell and Gash, 2007, Johnston et al., 2010, and Emerson et al., 2011). Implementation and significant outcomes are also needed to justify continued investment of resources, time and energy in collaborative governance regimes.

Conclusion

This chapter has summarised the key issues and findings covered by this book. Recommendations for addressing these issues include improving the backward and forward linkages between extractive industries and other industries for a more comprehensive and diversified industrial development and value addition in Africa. They also include strengthening institutions, policies and regulations and improving contracting, fiscal and revenue management systems to ensure that the wealth from extractive resources contribute to employment, income, improved living standards and inclusive growth in Africa. There is also the need to internalise environmental, health and social costs of the operations of extractive industries. The efficacy of implementing these recommendations and realising their intended outcomes could be improved with appropriate governance regime that could provide broad-based participation and transparent decision-making processes.

This chapter has also presented the relevant features that can facilitate these positive outcomes of collaborative governance regimes. It has discussed how collaborative governance could serve as the framework for a regime capable of addressing the critical issues such as transparency, accountability, decentralised and broader stakeholder participation in a contentious policy environment, such as that of extractive industries. It has provided some critical measures that should guide the design of the collaborative process. These include: having sponsor(s) with the capacity and resources to invest in collaborative governance

217

regimes, and; having leader(s) with the credibility, skills and expertise to initiative and manage the relationships and outcomes of multilateral decision-making. Within a collaborative governance regime, there should be formalised and institutionalised processes, as well as appropriate rules and protocols for stakeholder engagement. Stakeholders should be provided with the capacity, incentives and resources to enable them gain ownership, legitimacy and collective commitment to decision-making and implementation. Collaborative governance regimes can have several positive outcomes. These include the equitable distribution, access to and use of the wealth from extractive resources for inclusive growth and improved environmental management. These benefits should justify the investment of the resources, time and energy required for collaborative governance of the extractive industries in Africa.

References

Afful-Koomson, T. 2012. Governance challenges for promoting the green economy in Africa. In: DE Oliveira, J. A. P. (ed.) Green economy and good governance for sustainable development: Opportunities, promises and concerns. Tokyo: United Nations University Press.

Ansell, C. and Gash, A. 2007. Collaborative governance in theory and practice. Journal of Public Administration Research and Theory 18, 543–571.

Brunnschweiler, C. and Bulte, E. H. 2009. Natural resources and violent conflict: Resource abundance, dependence, and the onset of civil wars. Oxford Economic Papers 61, 651–674.

Chrislip, D. and Larson, C. E. 1994. Collaborative leadership: How citizens and civic leaders can make a difference. San Francisco, CA: Jossey-Bass.

Emerson, K., Nabatchi, K. and Balogh, S. 2011. An integrative framework of collaborative governance. Journal of Public Administration Research and Theory 22, 1 –29.

218

Fjelde, H. 2009. Buying peace? Oil wealth, corruption and civil war. Journal of Peace Research 46, 199–218.

Fung, A. 2002. Collaboration and countervailing power: Making participatory governance work. www.archonfung.net/papers /CollaborativePower2.2.pdf [Accessed 22 August 2012].

Futrell, R. 2003. Technical adversaliasm and participatory collaboration in the US. Chemical weapons disposal programme Science Technology and Human Values 28, 451–82.

Huxham, C. and Vangen, S. 2004. Doing things collaboratively: Realising the advantage or succumbing to inertia. Organisational Dynamics 33, 190–201.

Johnston, E. W., Hicks, D., Nan, N. and Auer, J. C. 2010. Managing the inclusion process in collaborative governance. Journal of Public Administration Research and Theory 21, 699–721.

Rudra, N. and Jensen, N. M. 2011. Globalisation and the politics of natural resources. Comparative Political Studies 44, 639–661.

Ryan, C. 2001. Leadership in collaborative policy-making: An analysis of agency roles in regulatory negotiations. Policy Sciences 34, 221–245.

www.ingramcontent.com/pod-product-compliance
Lightning Source LLC
Chambersburg PA
CBHW050641280326
41932CB00015B/2737